POLITICS IN WARTIME

BOOKS BY

A. J. P. TAYLOR

Politics in Wartime and Other Essays (1965)

The First World War (1963)

The Origins of the Second World War (1962)

The Trouble Makers (1957)

Englishmen and Others (1956)

Bismarck: the Man and the Statesman (1955)

The Struggle for Mastery in Europe, 1848–1918 (1954)
(THE OXFORD HISTORY OF MODERN EUROPE)

Rumours of Wars (1952)

From Napoleon to Stalin (1950)

The Habsburg Monarchy, 1809–1918 (1949)

The Course of German History (1945)

Germany's First Bid for Colonies, 1884–85 (1938)

The Italian Problem in European Diplomacy, 1847–49 (1934)

POLITICS

IN

WARTIME

and Other Essays

BY

A. J. P. TAYLOR

F.B.A.

ATHENEUM *NEW YORK*

1965

CONTENTS

I

II

PREFACE

SOME historians, it has been said, produce rich plum puddings; some produce dry biscuits. I produce dry biscuits, I hope with a pronounced flavour. I hope, too, that the flavour has improved with keeping. *Politics in the First World War* was given before the British Academy as the Raleigh lecture on History for 1959 and has previously appeared in the *Proceedings of the British Academy* for that year. *Lloyd George: Rise and Fall* was given before the University of Cambridge as the Leslie Stephen lecture for 1961 and has been previously published by the Cambridge University Press. *The War Aims of the Allies in the First World War* first appeared in *Essays Presented to Sir Lewis Namier* (published by Macmillan) which Richard Pares and I edited. I am grateful for permission to republish them. I also acknowledge with thanks the permission to republish other essays, given by the editors, publishers, and proprietors of *Encounter*, the *Guardian* (formerly the *Manchester Guardian*), the *Listener*, the *New Statesman*, the *Observer*, and *History Today*.

A.J.P.T.

PART I

I

POLITICS IN THE FIRST WORLD WAR

Raleigh Lecture on History, 1959

In 1920 General Groener, Ludendorff's successor and last Quartermaster-General of the Imperial army, wrote of the first World war: 'The German general staff fought against the English parliament.' The phrase is quoted and, to a large extent endorsed, in *Der deutsche Reichstag im Weltkriege*, a substantial volume laid before the Reichstag committee of inquiry into the causes of Germany's defeat by Dr. J. V. Bredt, himself a Democratic deputy. Dr. Bredt argues that the Reichstag played an important and occasionally decisive part during the war. If it did not shape German policy, this was its own fault, and that of the parties; the general staff gave way whenever it was faced by a parliamentary majority. Dr. Bredt looks sadly over to the enemy side across the Channel where things, he believes, were different. The British house of commons asserted civilian control; the German Reichstag did not. Hence the Allies won the war; hence the sentence of General Groener with which I began.

The defeated—both Reichstag and general staff—have received much attention from historians. Indeed German politics during the first World war are one of the few fields in recent history which is in danger of being over-worked. What did the British parliament and British politicians do during the first World war? The theme has been strangely neglected. Metternich's complaint against old Austria has become the guiding principle of English historians: 'administration has taken the place of government'. The machinery

11

of public authority has been studied, from the war cabinet down to local agricultural committees. Only one writer has presented 'a political history of the war'; and even he hesitated over the claim.[1] No word of mine should be taken as criticism of Lord Beaverbrook's splendid volumes. Their brilliant presentation, wealth of material and deep understanding of men's motives, stir the admiration of the professional historian, not his jealousy. But Lord Beaverbrook deals, as he says himself, with the Peaks of Politics, not with the general course of political events. Some of the great questions are passed over lightly, of intent. Thus of Ireland: 'The issue is dead, and it does not possess a spark of life or interest to the reader of to-day';[2] 'it would be unprofitable to dissect its lifeless body'.[3] Lord Beaverbrook adds in his usual disarming way: 'I am quite prepared to admit that I may be wrong in the small importance I now attach to these Irish stories.'[4] Again, conscription—the question which began the disintegration of the Liberal party—'was not a burning issue'. 'To trace all the ramifications of [the politicians'] beliefs would be tedious to the last degree.'[5] During the great moments of crisis as described by Lord Beaverbrook, the house of commons provides noises off; it never occupies the centre of the scene. This, though it may well be a true picture, merits examination. This lecture may be taken as a supplement to Lord Beaverbrook's work, or, in a phrase which he has used in a different connexion, 'another version of the same'.

The house of commons, elected in December 1910, was

[1] Lord Beaverbrook would have liked to call Volume One of *Politicians and the War* (1928) 'a Political History', but was 'only too well aware that the description would be a misnomer'. Volume Two (n.d.) 'does not profess to be a detailed history of the politics of the war'. In *Men and Power 1917–1918* (1956), however, he describes the two earlier volumes as 'an earnest attempt to provide an impartial political history'.

[2] *Politicians and the War*, i. 50.   [3] Ibid. ii. 64.   [4] Ibid. ii. 13.

[5] Ibid. i. 207, 206. But on ii. 44: 'A frank discussion and vote in the Cabinet would have broken the administration to pieces. . . . We find here the germ of a fundamental difference of view as to the aim of the War and the methods by which it was to be conducted which completely transcended party.'

indeed ill-prepared to direct, or even to influence, the conduct of a great war. The general election had been fought, to the boredom of the electorate, on the question of the house of lords. Thereafter the house plunged from one passionate party controversy to another. Foreign affairs were rarely discussed: less than in the parliament of 1906–10, and hardly at all after February 1912. In August 1914 all these great causes of controversy were dimmed. The house of lords had surprisingly reached a lasting settlement, or next door to it, in 1911. Irish Home Rule was pushed aside on the outbreak of war when the Home Rule Act, though placed on the statute book, was suspended for the duration. National Insurance had ceased to be contentious—duchesses had long been licking stamps; and Welsh Disestablishment no longer stirred a flame except in the Welsh and Lord Robert Cecil. Even the long-standing argument between free trade and tariff reform appeared irrelevant when set against the background of national survival. The House was united. All members, a bare half-dozen excepted, recognized the necessity of war in August 1914. The way seemed clear for the house to become a great Council of State.

The appearance of national unity was deceptive. There were still deep cleavages in the party outlooks. The Unionists, by and large, regarded Germany as a dangerous rival, threatening either the Balance of Power or Great Britain's imperial interests—maybe both together. They proposed to fight a hard-headed war by ruthless methods, and regarded any 'moral' advantage as a windfall. For the Liberals, this 'moral' advantage was essential. Many of them had come to support the war only when Germany invaded Belgium, and even the less radical among them were relieved to escape from a 'realistic' position. Entering the war for altruistic motives, the Liberals wished to conduct it by highminded means, and they found it harder to abandon their principles than to endure defeat in the field. There would have been raging conflict between the two parties if the profound difference of outlook had been brought into the open. The leaders of both were therefore anxious to keep it under cover.

The house heard a general oration from Asquith on 6 August and then adjourned on 10 August. It met for a brief session from 25 August to 17 September, solely to finish with Home Rule, and this caused bitterness enough. Then it met again on 11 November. In the nine months of Liberal rule Asquith gave one war survey, on 1 March 1915—a survey which did not mention the campaign in France; and no debate followed.[1]

This unspoken Coalition between the front benches was not new. The habit had been growing for some time, and the scenes in the House became increasingly artificial. The leaders met amicably at Round Table conferences at Buckingham Palace, still flushed from the passionate debates over the Parliament Bill or Home Rule. Even their disputes here were to some extent staged. The very men who failed to agree at the Palace negotiated secretly for a full Coalition, and were impeded only by their backbenchers. Austen Chamberlain, embarrassed as usual by his own honesty, remarked: 'What a world we live in and how the public would stare if they could look into our minds and our letter bags.'[2] Hilaire Belloc exercised his satirical imagination on this theme; but, as often happens, reality outdid the wildest flights of fantasy. There is nothing in *Pongo and the Bull* to rival the improbable scene in May 1915 when Bonar Law, making a morning call on Lloyd George, was conducted through a side-door to Asquith; whereupon the two men destroyed one government and made another within quarter of an hour. The war in fact provided the means of stilling party disputes which the leaders had failed to find for themselves.

There were other, less melodramatic, reasons why the house of commons was virtually ignored. For one thing, Kitchener, the secretary of state for war, sat in the lords. Here he surveyed the war, inadequately, about once a month,

---

[1] Churchill alone dissented from this policy of silence, and twice attempted to survey the war in broad terms (on 27 November 1914 and 15 February 1915). These attempts obviously embarrassed the House, though they set a pattern for the second World war; few members listened, and none followed Churchill's lead.

[2] Charles Petrie, *Austen Chamberlain*, i. 258.

but he did not allow the under-secretary to follow his example in the house of commons. It is indeed a minor oddity of the war that, until Lloyd George became prime minister, only the lords discussed broad questions of strategy; and one member, Lord Milner, openly defied the rules of security—to the bewilderment of the Germans.[1] Generally speaking, the Liberal government practised individual enterprise in politics as rigidly as in economic affairs. Each minister was left free to conduct his own department, and Asquith, acting as the detached chairman, intervened only when it was necessary to arbitrate between ministers. Here incidentally is the explanation, forgotten in later years, why Grey before the war consulted the cabinet little—and informed the house still less—on foreign policy. That was his department, and it was his job to run it. So, when the war began, the cabinet never approved the ultimatum to Germany; this was settled by Grey, perhaps with assistance from Asquith. The cabinet endorsed the dispatch of the Expeditionary Force to France only after this had begun, and their naming of an assembly point (Amiens instead of Maubeuge) was disregarded by the military authorities. The secrets of naval strategy were locked in Fisher's breast, from which they never emerged.

The prorogation on 17 September had behind it the assumption that the war would be lost or won before the house met again. By 11 November this assumption had been belied. Deadlock set in; a long war was in the offing. But this did not provoke any discussion in the house of commons. A new factor aided the policy of silence. The first World war produced an excessive enthusiasm for secrecy, or 'security' as it came to be called. There was something to be said for keeping shipping-movements and losses secret; though this was carried rather far when the sinking of the *Audacious*, which took place on 27 October 1914, was announced only on 13 November 1918. But it seems unlikely that the Germans

[1] Milner discussed the evacuation from Gallipoli a fortnight before it took place. The Germans concluded that this was a ruse, to cloak preparations for a further landing.

overlooked the presence of a British army in France. 'Security' operated more against the British public than against the enemy. The authorities, military and political, had no idea how to win the war; therefore they wished to keep silence until, by some miracle as yet unforeseen, the war was won. In theory reports of proceedings in parliament were free from censorship. This meant in practice that nothing could be mentioned in parliament which might infringe the requirements of 'security'. Questions were unofficially censored before they were set down; members were kept quiet by the appeal to patriotism.

The policy of silence might have worked if everyone outside the government could really ignore the war, if 'Business as Usual', in Churchill's phrase, really made sense. Quite the contrary. Where direction was lacking, enthusiasm had to take its place. For nearly a year and a half the army was raised by voluntary recruiting, which provided three out of every four men for the greatest armies ever put into the field by this country. The public had to be kept constantly astir by recruiting meetings; and, though ministers and members of parliament spoke a good deal, these meetings provided a platform for less official orators. Here Horatio Bottomley made his fame. Recovering from the discredit into which he had recently fallen, he rose before the end of the war to become the tribune of the people, respectfully consulted—not only according to his own account—by the war cabinet itself.

Silence in high places cleared the way for demagogues. Still more, it cleared the way for the masters of the press. The public wanted news, and could find it only in the newspapers. Official statements told nothing, and the alternative means of communication, developed later in the twentieth century, were as yet unknown. Soon too the public wanted leadership, and again only the newspapers provided it. The 'press lords' did not snatch at influence and power; these were thrust on them by the abdication of the politicians. Northcliffe, who controlled half the circulation in London, was the most notorious of these press lords, but he was not alone. Robert Donald, editor of the *Daily Chronicle*, played almost as great a part. C. P. Scott and J. L. Garvin were to join him as kingmakers in the great crisis of 1916.[1] The politicians railed and complained without ever appreciating that the fault lay in themselves. Lloyd George alone realized the true position. Always more at home on the public platform than in the house of commons and unfettered by traditional rules, he early recognised that public opinion must be satisfied somehow. He commented on 23 June 1916: 'The Press has performed the function which should have been performed by Parliament, and which the French Parliament has performed.'[2] Lloyd George used the press; and the press used Lloyd George. The two grew great together. Lloyd George had never cared much for the society of other politicians. Now he built up a group of advisers drawn almost entirely from the press. The chief of these were Riddell, who owned the *News of the World*; C. P. Scott of the *Manchester Guardian*; and Robertson Nicoll, editor of the *British Weekly*, a strong though tardy supporter of the war (like Lloyd George himself),[3] who could best interpret the feeling of the pro-war Dissenters. The only politician admitted to these gatherings was Addison, a Radical doctor from the East End, who had entered Parliament in 1910 and had worked with Lloyd George on National Insurance. Through these men Lloyd George gauged public opinion more effectively than by sitting regularly in his place in the house of commons.

Even so, feeling in parliament stirred under the surface. The backbench Unionists resented the unofficial coalition of silence to which Bonar Law had committed them. Early in 1915 some of them set up the Unionist Business Committee under the nominal leadership of Walter Long (once Bonar

[1] It is often implied that Max Aitken who was even more a king-maker in December 1916 also owed his power to the press. This is not so. Aitken only became a press lord in the decisive sense later.

[2] Riddell, *War Diary*, p. 151.

[3] On 1 August 1914 Lloyd George received from Nicoll a letter opposing entry into the war. He found it in the pocket of his dress-suit on 7 August and pinned it to Nicoll's pro-war leader of 5 August. Riddell, *War Diary*, p. 11.

Law's rival) to press—irrelevantly—for Tariffs. They were drawn instead into complaints against the inadequate supply of munitions; complaints which were seconded by the former auxiliaries of the Liberal government—the Irish Nationalists and Labour. This was a startling development. The Liberals and Unionists exactly balanced after the general election of 1910, but Asquith had a stable and substantial majority thanks to the Irish and Labour. These two held the balance, but only in appearance; for, while they could certainly put the Liberals out, it would have been intolerable for them to put the Unionists in. Hence Asquith could make more demands on them than they on him, simply by evoking the ghost of a Unionist administration. Labour slipped back into being Lib-Lab; and at each stage of the Home Rule crisis, the Irish were pushed from one concession to another as the price for getting anything at all. In August 1914 Asquith assumed that the two parties would continue their tame acquiescence, apart of course from the few Labour men who actually opposed the war, and he concerned himself more with the Ulstermen than with the Nationalists once Home Rule was technically on the statute book. This was one aspect, and by no means the least, of the fatal self-confidence which brought Asquith to ruin. He took it for granted that for the Irish and Labour (as for everyone else) he was the indispensable man.

For these two parties it soon ceased to be true. The Irish Nationalists had nothing to gain by supporting Asquith now that Home Rule was laid aside. On the contrary they had good reason to attack the Liberal government, or rather its outstanding member Kitchener, who had depreciated the surge of Irish loyalty by refusing to authorize an Irish Brigade.[1] With Labour it was the other way round. Far from being slighted, Labour—meaning the Labour movement and not merely the handful of Labour men in the House—was called into the seats of the mighty for the first time. The

[1] The Ulster Volunteers, on the other hand, got official recognition. Hence Carson and the Ulster Unionists supported Kitchener and even Asquith, as later they supported other military leaders. Carson indeed was the vital link between Asquith and the generals; a curious and yet appropriate position.

Treasury agreement of March 1915, and its ancillary agreements, made the trade unions partners in the industrial life of the country. It was hopeless thereafter to regard Labour as a mere auxiliary of the Liberal party. Both Labour and the Irish were feeling their way to independence, though for different reasons. Both wanted the war to be won— Labour because the working people of the country were fighting it, the Irish because of Redmond's belief that a victory for freedom abroad would bring freedom for Ireland also. Neither, however, cared particularly that Asquith should win it, still less Kitchener.

Both were ready to join the Unionist revolt. On 7 May 1915 the revolt exploded. During a debate on the Defence of the Realm Act, Redmond moved the adjournment of the house—ostensibly against state purchase of the liquor trade, really as a protest against its irrelevance to the shell shortage. The Unionist Business Committee were emboldened to draft an open motion on this subject. Bonar Law tried to head the rebels off. On 13 May, just before the House rose for the Whitsuntide recess, he sent a message to the Committee urging postponement. He thought he had succeeded. But Hewins, the real inspirer of the Committee, was unappeased. Hewins had been a Professor of Economics and, like most academics turned politician, combined high principles and impracticality in equal measure. On 17 May Hewins warned Bonar Law that he would force a debate on munitions when the House resumed. Bonar Law at first acquiesced, then asked Hewins to hold his hand. The next day Hewins learnt that the Liberal government had resigned and that a Coalition was being formed.

Bonar Law had not feared that the Unionist rebels would fail. He feared that they would succeed. Then, perhaps after a general election, 'there would have been a Conservative government which would have had to introduce conscription after terrible controversy'.[1] The Liberals would have become 'an ordinary party opposition with effects most disastrous to

[1] Bonar Law in the House of Commons, 4 April 1917; *Hansard*, 5th series, xcii. 1392.

the country'.[1] Ostensibly the crisis was provoked by
Fisher's resignation as first sea lord on 15 May, not by the
threat of Unionist revolt. This was a stroke of luck for Bonar
Law, enabling him to cloak the real danger; but the warning
from Hewins gave the decisive push which sent him on his
dramatic visit to Lloyd George. The first Coalition was
indeed made by parliamentary pressure, but it was created to
thwart this pressure, not to satisfy it. The only good result
of the crisis was the ministry of munitions, with Lloyd
George at its head. Otherwise the party leaders were more
in control than ever. Even the semblance of a front Opposition bench vanished. The discontented Unionists were unable
to appeal to public opinion; they were denied a conflict and a
general election which, according to Bonar Law himself, they
would have won; Liberal ministers kept the key posts;
so did Kitchener, the worst offender even in the eyes of his
Liberal colleagues; the Unionist recruits got the crumbs. The
manoeuvre was completed, the new government formed,
before parliament reassembled. The backbench Liberals
were equally dismayed. Their government—the last Liberal
government in British history as it turned out—was gone
without a word of explanation. Belatedly Asquith called the
Liberals together and appeased them with twenty minutes of
emotional explanation. 'Some of the members were moved to
tears as was the Prime Minister himself.'[2]

The Liberals did well to weep. Despite Asquith's rigging
of appointments, the Liberals were now taken prisoner in
their turn by 'national unity'. Previously Bonar Law had
kept the Unionists quiet so as not to embarrass the government; henceforward the Liberals had to acquiesce in unwelcome policies so as to maintain the Coalition. Thus in May
1916 Bonar Law wrote to Asquith: 'I believe that it is easier
for you to obtain the consent of your party to general
compulsion than for me to obtain the consent of my party to
its not being applied.'[3] Asquith did not understand the great

---

[1] So Bonar Law told Redmond: D. Gwynn, *Redmond*, p. 467.
[2] Addison, *Four and a Half Years*, i. 79.
[3] Bonar Law to Asquith, May 1916; Spender, *Life of Asquith*, ii. 211.

issues which the conduct of the war provoked. Though resolved on victory, he supposed that the only contribution statesmen could make was to keep out of the way, while free enterprise supplied the arms with which generals would win the battles. The only dividing line he recognized was the old one between tariff reform and free trade. Hence his overriding concern when making the Coalition was to put free traders at the exchequer and the board of trade. Even here his calculation went wrong. McKenna, chancellor of the exchequer, betrayed his own free trade convictions. With the financial rectitude of a born banker, McKenna introduced in September 1915 the first real war budget—a budget on which incidentally his successor Bonar Law did not improve; and this included, among other revolutionary innovations, the McKenna Duties, ostensibly designed to reduce imports, which were in fact Protection. Lloyd George appropriately threw a note across the cabinet table to Walter Long on 16 September: 'So the old system *goes* destroyed by its own advocates.'[1] The McKenna Duties produced one of the first divisions of the war. Ten Radicals voted against them on 1 October—a tiny number, yet a sign of the coming disintegration.

The dispute was, in the circumstances of war, a triviality, as the division showed. The great underlying conflict was between freedom and organization. Could the war be conducted by 'Liberal' methods—that is, by voluntary recruiting and by *laissez-faire* economics? Or must there be compulsory military service, control of profits, and direction of labour and industry? When the Coalition was being formed, Runciman wrote to McKenna:

If we are honoured with an invitation to come in I feel that we must first know with whom we are asked to associate . . . in particular . . . if they were told that we had an open mind on compulsory service or taxation.[2]

His question remained unanswered. But it was constantly pushed forward by the march of events. Of its two aspects—

[1] Hewins, *Apologia of an Imperialist*, ii. 52.
[2] S. McKenna, *Reginald McKenna*, p. 223.

conscription and the control of industry—the second was the more urgent. For at least a year ahead voluntary recruiting would in fact provide more men than free enterprise could equip. But economic direction was far more difficult to apply. Not only was it more alarming in theory. It was unwelcome to both Capital and Labour, yet it could not work without their consent. On paper the government had all it needed with the act setting up the ministry of munitions, or indeed with the Defence of the Realm Act. In practice these powers were ineffective unless industry accepted them. Lloyd George grasped this intuitively when he ended the strike in South Wales by agreeing to the miners' demands instead of by invoking legal sanctions as Runciman, at the board of trade, wished to do. It was no doubt illogical that men safely at home should kick against lesser sacrifices than those which they expected from the soldiers and which they would willingly make were they themselves in the trenches; but it was an inescapable fact.

Ministers and members of parliament alike felt that they were contending against H. G. Wells's 'Invisible Man'. Members demanded the enforcement of penalties and railed against the feebleness of ministers. Ministers could not understand their own helplessness and sought to turn the flank of this baffling problem. One such attempt, strangely enough, was Liquor Control—restricted hours for the opening of licensed premises. The question had been initiated by Lloyd George in the last days of the Liberal government when he had proposed State Purchase of the liquor trade—the first of his many attempts to find an inspiring cause that would sweep him to national leadership. Lloyd George aimed principally to recapture the allegiance of the Radical Dissenters—once his most solid backers—and to reconcile them no doubt to other, less welcome, war measures; he also hoped to establish his reputation as 'the man of push and go'—to borrow the phrase applied to a more forgotten figure, G. W. Booth—and so to dispel the remaining suspicions against his prewar Radicalism. State Purchase miscarried; and Lloyd George forgot it when he arrived at the ministry of munitions. But Liquor Control had the same dual purpose. Liberals (who in any case liked the idea for its own sake) could argue that working men would be industrious and productive, without direction of labour, once they were sober; Unionists of the planning school welcomed Liquor Control as the prelude to control of everything else. At least some Unionists did. Others, though equally 'planners', opposed it, and not merely from their long-standing connexion with 'The Trade.' They suspected, rightly, that it was a red herring, ostentatiously displayed to divert them from more serious quarry.

The Unionists answered by pressing for compulsory military service. No doubt many of them did so from simple impulse. They were after all simple men; and conscription was the obvious sentimental response to the situation, as Sir John Simon—one of its opponents at the time—recognized in later life. But conscription, too, was a red herring. There was little to be said in its favour from a military point of view. Sir Auckland Geddes, Director of National Service, said when all was over:

With, perhaps, more knowledge than most of the working of conscription in this country, I hold the fully matured opinion that, on balance, the imposition of military conscription added little if anything to the effective sum of our war efforts.[1]

The immediate effect of conscription was to stop voluntary recruiting, which ceased on 27 January 1916—the day when the first Military Service Act became law. Thereafter the compulsory system, far from bringing more men into the army, kept them out of it. Men in reserved occupations who were doing vital work could not be prevented from succumbing to patriotic enthusiasm so long as enlistment was voluntary. They stayed at their jobs once conscription went through. The figures prove it. There had been a great outcry in the autumn of 1915 that 650,000 single men were evading military service. When the Act was passed, it arranged

[1] The words have often been quoted. I take them from Simon, *Retrospect*, p. 107.

43,000 recruits in its first six months of operation (about
half the average number raised in a single month by the
voluntary system). Its more important result was to produce
748,587[1] fresh claims to exemption, most of them valid.[1]
This was not at all what the simple-minded enthusiasts for
conscription had expected. More clearsighted Unionists were
unperturbed. They were content either way. If compulsion
produced millions of fresh soldiers, then their needs would
overwhelm the 'free' economic system. Alternatively if it produced only claims for reservation, industrial conscription was
being attained by the back-door.

These considerations were appreciated on the Liberal side.
The strictest Liberals opposed any hint of conscription,
military or industrial. The proposal to set up even a National
Register produced the first division of the war on 5 July 1915,
when 30 voted in the minority. Sir John Simon resigned from
the government at the end of the year, thus drawing on a
stock of moral inflexibility that was not much replenished
later, and 105 votes were cast against the Military Service
Bill for single men on 5 January 1916—50-odd Liberals when
the Irish are deducted. Others, including Pringle—later an
assiduous 'wee free'—acquiesced, however, when they were
assured that industrial conscription would not follow.
McKenna and Runciman took this line inside the cabinet. On
29 December 1915 they, too, determined to resign; then
thought better of it and stayed in the cabinet to thwart the
economic effects of conscription, which they did with marked
effect. Runciman especially remained a rigid free trader at
the board of trade, and his helplessness in face of shipping
losses produced on 9 November 1916 what Addison described
as 'the most invertebrate and hopeless of any memoranda
presented to the Government during the war by a responsible
head of a department on a great issue'.[2] By the autumn of
1916 economic liberalism was played out. The only logical
alternatives were to abandon liberalism or to abandon the
war. Hence the cry for 'peace by negotiation', first faintly

[1] *Military Operations: France and Belgium 1916*, i. 152.
[2] Addison, *Politics from Within*, ii. 10.

heard in November 1915 and raised even within the cabinet a year later. But on the whole this cry came only from those who had opposed the war all along. Most Liberals drifted in the wake of Asquith, their leader, trapped like him by the decision of August 1914. They had willed the end, but would not will the means.

This great conflict was not confined to the house of commons nor even to the press. It was voiced also by the demagogues of the recruiting platform. Uninstructed public opinion agreed with the Unionists in clamouring for military conscription. On the other hand it agreed with the Liberals in opposing any sort of economic interference or control. This was shown when Independent candidates first appeared in defiance of the electoral truce. The truce remained unbroken until December 1915, except in the anomalous instance of Merthyr Boroughs, vacant by the death of Keir Hardie, where the 'official' pacifist, nominated by the I.L.P., was beaten by a pro-war Labour man. The first real breach came at Cleveland on 10 December 1915. Here Bottomley and his Business Government League ran a local publican on the combined ticket of compulsory military service and no liquor control. Bottomley, himself disreputable, attracted only disreputable supporters. Pemberton Billing was a more formidable and more successful campaigner. In January 1916 he almost won Mile End; on 10 March he captured East Hertfordshire from a Unionist. To the usual popular demands for a free liquor trade and universal conscription, he made an addition of his own: 'a strong air policy'. The Zeppelin raids had begun, and Pemberton Billing, voicing the demand for reprisals, became the one and only 'Member for Air'. It seems odd that he should defeat a Unionist, but this conformed to the general rule: official Unionists always did worse at by-elections than official Liberals, and for a topsyturvy reason. Unionist voters were contented with the Coalition and therefore supported the official Liberal when they had no nominee of their own. Liberals resented the Coalition and voted for the independent candidate, however eccentric, who received time and again roughly the Liberal poll of 1910.[1] The Liberals felt that they were being dragged further and further away from Liberalism; the Unionists complained only that the process was not going on fast enough. Ultimately the two complaints co-incided to cause the crisis of December 1916.

Before this, there was to be a last display of Asquith's virtuosity. Asquith developed over conscription all the tactical hesitations which had bedevilled Home Rule, waiting for events to enforce the solution which he himself could not impose nor even foresee. He had no policy of his own, only a desire to keep the Unionists in without driving the Liberals out. First he postponed decision by the Derby scheme— presenting attestment to the Liberals as a device for evading conscription, to the Unionists as its preliminary. In January 1916 he accepted conscription for single men, again appeasing Liberals by a reminder of all the married men who would escape. The demand for general conscription continued to grow, and on 19 April Asquith expected the Government to break up. He devised another elaborate compromise which satisfied neither party, and on 26 April presented this scheme to the House in the first secret session of the war. The secrecy was imposed in order to conceal the party rifts from the public, not to deny knowledge to the enemy. Asquith had a stroke of luck—his last. 26 April was the Tuesday after Easter. On the previous day Dublin had broken into revolt. The house, too, revolted. In a surge of patriotism, it deman-ded a final, comprehensive measure; and this demand grew

[1] Contested by-elections in 1916, with programme of unofficial candidate. *January*: West Newington: Independent against the Liquor Control Board. Mile End: Pemberton Billing (almost successful) against the Liquor Control Board and for air-raid reprisals. *March*: East Hertford-shire: Pemberton Billing, successful. Hyde: Independent against the Liquor Control Board and for conscription. Market Harborough: Independent for conscription. *April*: Wimbledon: Kennedy Jones, 'Do it Now'. *May*: Tewkesbury: Independent for strong War Council. *August*: Berwick: an Independent called Turnbull on whom I have no information. *September*: Mansfield: Turnbull again. *October*: North Ayrshire: 'Peace by Negotiation' candidate. Winchester: Independent was merely descri-bed as 'author and journalist'. The disappearance of pro-war Independent candidates after the passing of general conscription is striking. I have not included Irish by-elections, which shed no light on British politics.

even stronger three days later when the news arrived that Kut had surrendered to the Turks. Asquith gave a sigh of relief. He withdrew his compromise, carried universal military service, and yet preserved the unity of the government.

This was a triumph of tactics, however undeserved. But it was disastrous for Asquith's prestige. Everyone knew that the solution had been imposed upon him. The house had intervened effectively for the only time in the war; it had dictated to the Government instead of being led. Moreover there was a price to pay. Asquith had escaped an explosion over conscription only by raising the yet darker shadow of Ireland. Now he attempted to retrieve his reputation by 'solving' the Irish question. He crossed dramatically to Dublin. Then, as usual, he shrank from the creative effort that a 'solution' would imply. There was someone eager to take his place. Lloyd George had come near to resignation in protest against the delays over conscription, and had been urged to it by Scott and Robertson Nicoll. He had been deterred by a message from the king,[1] and perhaps more by his reluctance ever to carry out the threat of resignation. But his advocacy of conscription was known, and he had lost the favour of 'that crowd'—his former Radical supporters. Ireland was the way to regain it, and to eclipse Asquith as well. Lloyd George came nearer to solving the Irish question than anyone had ever done; secured agreement, by means however equivocal, between Carson and Redmond. The unity and confidence of the Liberal party seemed restored; that of the Unionists endangered. Bonar Law cared much for Ulster, little for the rest of Ireland. When Hewins complained that the proposed Irish settlement would break the Conservative party, Bonar Law replied pugnaciously: 'Perhaps the Conservative party has to be broken.'[2]

Once more Asquith wasted this great opportunity. The approval of Bonar Law, a mere iron-merchant from Glasgow, meant nothing to him, but he started back in alarm at

[1] Riddell, *War Diary*, p. 170.
[2] Hewins, *Apologia of an Imperialist*, ii. 81.

opposition from Lansdowne, a great Whig aristocrat, though of trifling weight in the Unionist party. The Irish settlement was abruptly jettisoned. The failure did Asquith incalculable harm. It lost him the last scrap of support from the Irish Nationalists. It shook his position inside the Liberal party; for, though Liberals might be in two minds over conscription, most felt strongly about Home Rule. Addison reflected this opinion when he wrote of Asquith: 'His conduct of this business had more to do with determining the attitude of many Liberals, including myself, than any other circumstance.'[1] Asquith used a favourite manœuvre to cover his retreat. He distracted attention from his failure over Ireland by agreeing, on 20 July, to a committee of inquiry into the campaign in Mesopotamia and threw in, for good measure, an inquiry into the Dardanelles as well. Such inquiries had in the past clearly displayed the power of the House—the inquiry into the Walcheren campaign, for example, in 1809 and, most assertive of all, the inquiry into the conduct of the Crimean war. These past inquiries had been forced on a reluctant government by the house—the Crimean inquiry brought the government down. The inquiries of 1916 were offered to the house as substitutes for real action: raking over dead campaigns instead of facing the great undecided question of economic direction. When the house accepted them, this was not a proof of its power, merely a sign that the crisis over conscription was exhausted.

For the moment the life seemed to go out of political controversy. There were no more Independent candidates at by-elections, demanding a more energetic conduct of the war. Few members listened to Winston Churchill on 22 August when he preached the doctrine of full War Socialism: rationing, direction of industry, industrial conscription. Still fewer applauded. Lloyd George, unexpectedly translated to the war office by the death of Kitchener forgot Home Rule as he had forgotten State Purchase, and now hoped to establish his fame by the simple expedient of winning the war. He said on 22 August: 'We are pressing the enemy back. . . . We

[1] Addison, *Politics from Within*, i. 260.

are pushing the enemy on the Somme. . . . He has lost his tide.'[1] A month later he committed himself to the knock-out blow. He was to make out later that he had done this in order to anticipate Wilson's proposal for a negotiated peace.[2] In fact he championed the knock-out blow because he supposed that, as secretary of state for war, he was himself about to deliver it. He had believed what Robertson and Haig told him. Hence his annoyance with them when their prophecies proved wrong; hence, too, his brisk publicising of this annoyance—he had to erase the memory of his own confident prophesying. In the autumn of 1916, with failure on the Somme, the inexorable question again raised its head: *laissez-faire* or controls? This time it could not be diverted by the irrelevant controversy over military conscription. Economic liberalism was on its last legs. Food, shipping, coal, manpower, all clamoured for control. Asquith talked action, did nothing.

The stage was set for a new Unionist revolt, this time against Bonar Law. The occasion seems a triviality, as Lord Beaverbrook and other writers have pointed out: the debate of 8 November over the disposal of enemy property in Nigeria. Yet even this was an appropriate symbol of the difference in outlook between idealistic Liberal and hard-headed Unionist. The Unionist rebels wanted to confine the sale of this enemy property to British subjects; the government, on Liberal principles, to dispose of it according to free trade rules. Sixty-five Unionists voted against the government, only seventy-three for it. The moment had almost arrived at which Bonar Law must leave the government or split the party. He talked of destroying the rebels at a general election, and Beaverbrook takes this threat seriously. It was surely empty, as Bonar Law must have known. The Unionists in the country were ahead of the rebels in parliament. The rogue candidates of the spring had become official Unionist candidates by the autumn. Kennedy Jones, for example, fought Wimbledon in April with the cry, 'Do

---

[1] *Hansard*, 5th series, lxxxv. 2556.
[2] Lloyd George, *War Memoirs*, ii. 851–9.

it Now'. In December he was returned unopposed as official
Unionist at Hackney. A general election would not have
destroyed the rebels; it would have returned them in greater
force. Bonar Law could save the Unionist party, and in
particular his own leadership of it, only by destroying the
Asquith government. In this sense, the division of 8 November was the decisive event of the war so far as the British
house of commons was concerned. It set the train to the mine
which brought down Asquith and put Lloyd George in his
place.

But it was only the beginning. Bonar Law could destroy the
Coalition. What would be its successor? Why not a predominantly Liberal government such as had existed until
May 1915? The answer could not be determined by the
Unionists. It rested with the Liberals themselves and with
their former associates. One striking change, though little
perceived at the time, was the gradual estrangement of these
satellites. The Irish Nationalists had lost all faith in Asquith
after his feebleness over Home Rule in the summer. Moreover, despite their insistence on Irish members remaining at
Westminster in full strength, they had unconsciously
abandoned the Union; and henceforward acted only when
Irish interests were affected—especially over the extension
of conscription to Ireland. But this was a negative development: 80 supporters lost to Asquith, not found by anyone else.
The transformation in regard to Labour was more positive.
The Labour movement grew more self-confident with each
day of the war. 'Labour' supported Asquith so long as he was
there, and even on 1 December Henderson called him 'the
indispensable man'. Yet essentially Labour did not care
about Asquith as against any other leader. They were only
interested in winning the war. In December 1916 the Labour
party came of age. The moment can be precisely defined: it
was the meeting of Liberal ministers on 4 December which
advised Asquith not to cooperate with Lloyd George.
Henderson attended the meeting, no doubt regarding himself and being regarded by others as one of Asquith's humbler
followers. Then in a flash of blinding truth he declared

(much to his own surprise) that Labour would support any prime minister who got on with the war, and a couple of days later he was in the war cabinet—no longer a Lib-Lab hanger-on, but spokesman of an independent Labour movement.

Still, a Unionist government, sustained only by Labour votes, would have been a shaky affair and would have brought with it the revival of party strife which Bonar Law dreaded. The position could be changed only by a Liberal split. Lloyd George himself could not provide this. He had powerful elements of the Liberal press on his side—both the *Daily Chronicle* and the *Manchester Guardian*; he had other prominent journalists backing him as the saviour of the country—Burnham, Geoffrey Dawson, Garvin, to say nothing of Northcliffe; he had even the support at this time of the military leaders from Robertson to Henry Wilson. But he had no contact with the Liberal rank and file in the house of commons. He knew few of them, and never tried to extend his personal influence. His political actions were shaped by intuition and by the advice of journalists—Riddell or Robertson Nicoll—who claimed to know public opinion. At this moment knowledge of public opinion was not enough. A new government had to count votes. The counting was done with decisive results by Christopher Addison, the one man in Lloyd George's intimate circle who was also in the house of commons. Addison had already taken a preliminary sounding during the critical days over conscription earlier in the year. On Monday, 4 December, he began canvassing the Liberal members more systematically. He soon reported that 49 Liberals supported Lloyd George unconditionally; by Wednesday, 6 December, he had found 126 who would support Lloyd George if he could form a government.[1] By this canvass Addison became the real maker of the Lloyd George government. The Unionist rebels forced Bonar Law into action. Max Aitken brought Lloyd George and Bonar Law together. It was Addison, and the Liberal rebels, who put Lloyd George in the first place.

[1] These are speculative figures. Lloyd George gives 136 in all as his supporters.

The Liberal split, which in fact ended the great Liberal party for ever, was more than a split over the conduct of the war. It revealed a deep division within the party which had been long a-growing. The Liberal leaders, associated with Asquith, were 'patricians': Asquith himself, 'last of the Romans', Crewe, Grey, Harcourt, McKenna—men of almost excessive culture and refinement. The supporters of Lloyd George were lower-class in origin, in temperament, in position. As an historian I rely more on feel than on figures, but I ran over the brief biographies which *The Times* appended to the successful candidates in the general election of 1918, and these confirmed my impression. Most of the Lloyd George Liberals were businessmen who had founded their own firms or were running a firm still with their family name. *The Times* says of one what could have been said of nearly all: 'a fine example of the self-made man'. The firms were all in wool or engineering, and no doubt doing well out of the war. None of these Liberals was a banker, merchant, or financial magnate. Those who were professional men also belonged to the second eleven: solicitors, not barristers; school teachers, not schoolmasters (a term reserved by *The Times* for those who taught at public schools). Hardly any had been educated at Oxford or Cambridge.[1] They were nearly all Nonconformists—usually Methodists—often the sons of Nonconformist ministers. Many of them had been keen Land Taxers before the war. In short, they resembled Lloyd George in everything except his genius. Their political ability was low; all they had was impatience with the arrogance and incompetence of the Asquith group. None made a serious mark on public affairs, and Lloyd George found it hard to recruit ministers from among them. Addison was the ablest of them, a proof how secondrate they were.

Still, Addison and these second-rank Liberals made Lloyd George prime minister. Bonar Law recognized Addison's

[1] Even the rare exceptions to these generalizations had something exceptional about them. Gordon Hewart, though a barrister, began as a journalist and went to the Bar late. H. A. L. Fisher, though a fellow of New College, was vice-chancellor of Sheffield University when invited to join Lloyd George's government.

crucial importance when he fired the mine on 28 November by asking: 'One cannot go on like this, Addison, do you think?'[1] Lloyd George had often threatened to resign—over munitions, over Gallipoli, over conscription, over his restricted powers at the War Office. He had always dodged away at the last moment. No doubt it was more difficult for him to dodge on 4 December when Asquith turned against him, but the preliminary information coming in from Addison also made it unnecessary. By 6 December Lloyd George had a cast-iron guarantee in his pocket that he alone could be prime minister: the Unionist rebels ruled out Asquith, the Liberal rebels would not have Bonar Law. It must have given him considerable amusement to watch first Asquith and then Bonar Law stubbing their toes on the submerged rock of the backbenchers. For Lloyd George's government sprang much more directly from parliamentary feeling than Asquith's coalition had done. The first Coalition was made against parliamentary discontent, to silence and thwart it; the second Coalition owed its existence to parliamentary discontent, which dictated to Bonar Law as much as against Asquith. The second Coalition was not a deal between the leaders of the two parties. Rather it was a defeat for all the leaders except Lloyd George, a defeat for the 'Three C's' as much as for the 'Squiffites', a defeat even for Bonar Law despite his tactical change of course at the last moment. The backbenchers represented a sort of unconscious plebiscite to make Lloyd George dictator for the duration of the war.

Lloyd George himself looked beyond party and parliament. He did not address the Unionist M.P.s. He never attended a meeting of his own Liberal supporters until after the armistice, and then did not know what to say to them. His only speech, on becoming prime minister, was to 'Labour'—that is, to a joint meeting of the Labour M.P.s and the national executive. Ramsay MacDonald surmised that Lloyd George planned to become leader of the Labour party. A shrewd guess, but not shrewd enough. Lloyd George

[1] Addison, *Four and a Half Years*, i. 269.

planned to become leader of 'the people', and Labour was merely one instrument to this end. His disregard of party came out clearly when he chose the war cabinet. When the government was being formed, Addison and Carson allotted the jobs under Bonar Law's eye—the one speaking for the Coalition Liberals, the other for the Unionists. Yet neither was included in the war cabinet. Instead Lloyd George put in men of no party weight: Milner and, later, Smuts. Even Curzon counted for little with the Unionists in the House of Commons. Only Labour, the smallest party of the Coalition in numbers, had a more or less official representative in the war cabinet, Arthur Henderson. Again, Lloyd George made no attempt to build up a Coalition Liberal organization. Addison repeatedly complained about this.[1] He supposed that Lloyd George could not devise a party programme. This was true, but it was still truer that Lloyd George would not even try: he wanted neither a programme nor organized backing. He preferred to keep the Coalition Liberals as individuals with no leaders except himself. He soon humiliated Addison and divorced him from the Coalition Liberals.[2] Their other spokesmen on joint committees with the Unionists, such as the committee on Home Rule, were Gordon Hewart and H. A. L. Fisher, both singularly unrepresentative.

Lloyd George made no secret of his intentions when he first addressed the house as prime minister on 19 December 1916. Parliamentary government, as it had been known for the last century or so, ceased to exist. A war cabinet without departmental or party ties would run all the affairs of the country; businessmen would head the important ministries

[1] He records these complaints in his diary on 12 April, 15 October, 21 November, 28 December 1917. In the end Lloyd George paid a penalty. He had few candidates ready for the general election of December 1918 and so was taken captive by the Unionists.

[2] In June 1917 Lloyd George made out (quite falsely) that he had had to intervene in the engineers' strike and clear up the mess made by Addison, as minister of munitions. Once Addison was safely shunted to the ministry of reconstruction, Lloyd George put the blame for the misrepresentation on his press-officer.

instead of politicians; and there would be 'a franker and fuller recognition of the partnership of Labour'—meaning that Lloyd George would address the T.U.C., not the house of commons, when he wished to speak to 'the people'. Lloyd George carried out his threats. He rarely appeared in the house of commons, leaving its leadership to Bonar Law —the first commoner prime minister to separate the two functions. The war cabinet submitted its annual reports for 1917 and 1918 direct to the nation without even inviting debate in the house of commons. At least one of the leading ministers, Sir Joseph Maclay, never entered the house. And in January 1918 Lloyd George defined British war aims in a speech to trade union leaders, not to the house of commons. The House was not browbeaten into impotence. It acquiesced. The backbenchers had confidence that Lloyd George would win the war and, having this confidence, insisted that he be left alone.

Lloyd George had another asset, perhaps an even greater one: the Opposition. Its existence was something new: there had been no Opposition since May 1915. Asquith made out that his function was independent support for the government as Bonar Law's had been in the first nine months of the war. But there was an essential difference. Bonar Law sustained the Liberal government against his own rank and file; Asquith hoped to destroy the Lloyd George government so far as he hoped for anything. What difference of principle divided the Opposition from the government? The great issue of *laissez-faire* or controls was settled—dictated by events as much as by policy; soon not even Runciman was denouncing convoys or rationing. The obvious course was to support Peace by Negotiation, since Lloyd George's was pre-eminently a war government. But Asquith never touched it, despite repeated alarms that he would do so. On the contrary, Lloyd George was pinned to relentless prosecution of the war for fear that Asquith would re-emerge as the war leader if he weakened. Peace by Negotiation certainly looked up in the course of 1917. It was carried to a division more than once; it was stimulated later in the year by the Lansdowne

letter; it produced candidates at three by-elections, all
of whom did badly.[1] None of the support came from the
'official' Opposition. They were even more hostile to it in
the house than the government benches; and in their
anxiety not to be tarred with Peace by Negotiation, failed even
to formulate war aims, abandoning this opening first to
Labour and then to Lloyd George himself.

An Opposition in wartime might have been expected to
claim that it could run the war better than the existing
Government. This claim was so grotesque in view of what
had gone before that Asquith never dared to make it. In his
usual fashion, he drifted, waiting for an issue to turn up; and
what turned up was defence of the generals against interference by the politicians. There was no principle behind this:
no man had more cause than Asquith to resent the interference of generals in politics. His support of them sprang
from lethargy, that fatal reluctance to lead which had brought
him down. He had ruined himself as prime minister by
sheltering behind Kitchener. 'If it had not been for Kitchener,
Asquith might have gone right through the war',[2] according
to Bonar Law. Equally he ruined his Liberal followers by
backing Robertson and Haig. The best chance of discrediting
the government came with the wasted victory at Cambrai—
the only victory in the war for which the church bells were
rung. But Asquith and his followers were saddled with their
devotion to Haig and made nothing of it. The outcry in
parliament came from a strange coalition of Kennedy Jones,
the 'Do It Now' Unionist, Joseph King, advocate of Peace by
Negotiation, and David Davies, a former associate of Lloyd
George's. They were told that Haig had made an inquiry and
that Smuts was making a further inquiry for the war
cabinet. The result of these inquiries was never published;
and this was perhaps as well. For they reached the compla-
cent, though not surprising, conclusion that 'no one down to
and including the corps commanders was to blame'; the fault

---

[1] Rossendale, 13 February; Stockton on Tees, 30 March; South
Aberdeen, 3 April 1917.
[2] Riddell, *War Diary*, p. 234.

lay with the regimental officers and the other ranks.[1] It was
a conclusion worthy of Asquith himself.

The Liberal Opposition indeed stood only for the principle
that Asquith was divinely appointed to go on being prime
minister for ever. This principle was enough to scare even
the most discontented back on to the side of Lloyd George.
Asquith often seemed to be on the point of splitting the
Unionists, as Lloyd George had split the Liberals. Each time
the Unionists cowered into silence at the question—Asquith
or Lloyd George as prime minister? For instance, many
Unionists resented the apparent predominance of press lords
in Lloyd George's administration. Austen Chamberlain
voiced this resentment with the backing of the Unionist War
Committee. To his dismay he was applauded by the Opposition Liberals and at once repudiated their support. 'They
and I do not act from the same motives or pursue the same
objects. I have tried from the first . . . to support the
Government of the day in carrying the War to a successful
conclusion. When these hon. Gentlemen can say the same,
and not before, shall I desire their cheers or their approval.'[2]
The applause indeed so horrified Austen Chamberlain that
not only did he drop his attack. Within a month he joined the
war cabinet and accepted the press lords as his colleagues.

The same story was repeated even more dramatically
during the series of disputes between Lloyd George and the
generals during the spring of 1918. The danger seemed
menacing. Asquith espoused the cause of the generals; it was
backed even more emphatically by Carson and the Die Hard
Tories. Yet essentially the danger was unreal. The Die Hards
would not dethrone Lloyd George, if this meant restoring
Asquith. On the eve of the Maurice debate, which was
expected to destroy Lloyd George, Carson attended the
Unionist War Committee, and reported sadly: 'Their hate
of Asquith overrides all other considerations, and they will
not back him to-morrow.'[3] So it proved. Even Carson voted

---

[1] *Military Operations: France and Belgium 1917*, iii. 296.
[2] 11 March 1918; *Hansard*, 5th series, civ. 77.
[3] Repington, *The First World War*, ii. 298.

for the Government. Only Asquith and 97 Liberals went into the Opposition lobby.[1] The division was indeed an historic occasion—the only time in the war when the official Opposition promoted a vote against the Government. But it was merely a political manœuvre, not a parliamentary revolt. Far from reasserting the authority of parliament, it made Lloyd George secure as he had never been before.

Asquith's leadership of the Opposition sustained Lloyd George in the country even more than in the house. Opposition was renewed at by-elections in the autumn of 1917 after the military failures of that year; but it was opposition demanding more vigorous measures, both military and economic, not the overthrow of Lloyd George. Ben Tillett, the only rogue candidate to repeat Pemberton Billing's success and get in, had an Asquithite as his 'official' rival at North Salford on 2 November. Tillett adroitly combined Labour and Die Hard extremism. His programme: vigorous prosecution of the war; better pay for soldiers and sailors; more direct Government control of the necessaries of life; anti-profiteering of food; and air-raid reprisals on a large scale. There was no grist here for Asquith's mill. Again the famous 'Black Book' which symbolized popular loss of faith in the governing classes contained the names of Mr. and Mrs. Asquith, so far as a non-existent Book can be said to contain anything; it did not contain the name of Lloyd George. Incidentally, Darling, the judge who conducted the case, though he could hardly believe in the Black Book (since this was said to contain his own name also) obviously thought that there was something in Pemberton Billing's allegations —striking evidence of the widespread contemporary hysteria. Pemberton Billing's last fling was to demand the internment of all enemy aliens. This nearly brought victory to his candidate at Clapham on 21 June 1918; it also produced a monster petition with a million and a half signatures, backed by the lord mayor of London. The proposal was even more

[1] The total vote against the Government was 106. The others were Irish Nationalists and anti-war Labour.

abhorrent to Asquith and his followers than to Lloyd George.[1]

Asquith could not reverse Lloyd George's feat and split the Unionists. Could he rival his other accomplishments? Could he win back Labour? Or reunite the Liberals? Labour ought to have given him a chance. The Labour leaders had no great trust in Lloyd George and no affection at all for the profiteers round him. Moreover in the summer of 1917 Henderson left the war cabinet over the affair of the Stockholm conference. This did not revive his allegiance to Asquith. He had seen too much of Asquith as head of a cabinet; besides the Liberal Opposition gave him no support when he was in trouble. Instead Henderson resolved to make Labour the second party in the state. Stockholm set in train a development which ultimately ruined all Liberals, the supporters of Lloyd George and Asquith alike. Between July 1917 and the end of the war Henderson created the modern Labour party. Labour continued to support the war, and the Labour ministers other than Henderson remained in office. At the same time Henderson formulated Labour's own foreign policy, with MacDonald's assistance, and so secured the future backing of the idealists. More important still, he enlisted Sidney Webb to transform the programme and organisation of the party so as to make it national instead of a sectional interest. The Labour party was standing on its own feet even

[1] Contested by-elections during the Lloyd George Coalition. 1917. *February*: Rossendale: peace by negotiation. *March*: Stockton on Tees: peace by negotiation. *April*: South Aberdeen: one Independent Nationalist; one Peace by Negotiation. *June*: Liverpool (Abercromby division): candidate backed by 'Discharged Soldiers' Federation' against the son of the secretary of state for war. *July*: South Monmouthshire: Prohibitionist. West Dundee: Prohibitionist. *October*: East Islington: town clerk of Hertford, a 'Vigilante', backed by Pemberton Billing; a 'National' candidate backed by Page-Croft. *November*: North Salford: Ben Tillett—successful.

1918. *February*: Prestwich: Cooperative candidate. *April*: Keighley: Peace by Negotiation. A woman candidate was also nominated but her papers were declared invalid. *May*: South Hereford: Farmers' Union. Wansbeck: Labour candidate, almost successful. *June*: Gravesend: one Independent Coalition; one Independent (pro-war) Labour. Clapham: Vigilante, backed by Pemberton Billing—'intern the lot'. *July*: East Finsbury: Vigilante, backed by Pemberton Billing, 'intern the lot'; Liquor Trade Independent—'boycott German shipping'.

before the war ended. At Wansbeck on 29 May 1918 a
Labour candidate, with the backing of the national party,
almost defeated the Coalition nominee. The writing was on
the wall. Labour had staked its claim to the front Opposition
bench, and soon Asquith would be pushed off it.

The only remaining expedient for Asquith was to reunite
the Liberal party. This was Lloyd George's most vulnerable
spot. He could not remain prime minister if he lost his
Liberal supporters, and the threat was the graver because it
did not necessarily imply the return of Asquith. The Unionists might achieve the dream of forming their own war
government. Yet Lloyd George remained cut off from the
Coalition Liberals, as he had been before Addison stamped
them out of the ground. They had no party organisation in
the country, and little even in the House. The Coalition
Liberal Whips were always vague who the whip should go
to, and even in the general election of 1918 the only definition of a Coalition Liberal was negative: a Liberal who did
not vote for the motion of inquiry after the Maurice debate.
Where party discipline was lacking, 'influence' had to take
its place. Hence the sale of honours which Lloyd George
conducted on an unprecedented scale. Of course Lloyd
George, having to build up a fund in two years where the
traditional parties had had half a century, was keen to sell,
and the Coalition Liberals, having no social position and
much easily-won money, were eager to buy. But such
transactions were the only way in which Lloyd George could
hold his followers together.

Still 'influence' was not enough. The Coalition Liberals
could not altogether forget their Radical and Nonconformist
origins. Even 'George's bloody knights' of Northcliffe's
deadly phrase might respond to a clear Liberal call. Lloyd
George rushed into this battle whenever challenged, quite
contrary to his ordinary disregard of parliament. Where
Asquith had told critics to wait and see, Lloyd George never
waited, and as a result his critics never saw. Asquith could
not recover Liberal allegiance as the alternative warleader.
But someone else might. The gravest threat came from

Churchill, excluded from Lloyd George's government on Unionist insistence and now sitting with the Liberals on the front Opposition bench. On 10 May 1917 Lloyd George held a secret session, apparently to prepare the way for direction of labour and food control. He made an effective speech, but it was Churchill who dominated the House. Lloyd George did not waste a moment. He caught Churchill behind the Speaker's chair while the debate was still in progress and, says Churchill, 'assured me of his determination to have me at his side. From that day, although holding no office, I became to a large extent his colleague.'[1] Two months later Churchill became minister of munitions. The Unionists protested, from Bonar Law downwards; but they could do nothing, short of going over to Asquith. It was safer to offend them than to run the risk that the Liberals might reunite. The operation had the additional satisfaction for Lloyd George of sending Addison from munitions to the impressive obscurity of reconstruction: another potential rival out of the way.

The same preoccupation with Liberal feeling was shown when Lloyd George made one of his rare appearances in the House to defend the shortlived ban on sending the *Nation* abroad. This ban, though indefensible, seems a trivial matter to have brought the prime minister down to the house at a critical moment of the war. But the *Nation* was a revered Liberal paper, despite its advocacy of a negotiated peace; revered especially by the former Radicals who now supported Lloyd George. In this case Lloyd George evaded danger by retreating in a cloud of words. The conscientious objectors showed his other method. Sympathy might have been expected from one who had been virtually a conscientious objector in a previous war. On the contrary, once Lloyd George abandoned principle, no one else was allowed to keep it, and he carried his Radical supporters with him simply by imitating Bottomley or Pemberton Billing: 'I will make the path of these men a very hard one.' Bonar Law showed more sympathy to the conscientious objectors, and it was left to

[1] Churchill, *World Crisis, 1916–1918*, i. 255.

Lord Hugh Cecil to divide the house against their disfran-
chisement—losing only by 171 to 209. The minority included
a number of those usually counted as Coalition Liberals.

Ireland was Lloyd George's real worry rather than the
generals or even the Germans. For one thing he owed his
position largely to the belief of many Liberals that he would
have solved the Irish question, had Asquith not let him down;
and he was therefore almost driven into another attempt at
solution now that he was in supreme command. But what he
has written about his handling of Haig and Robertson applies
also to his Irish policy: 'I never believed in costly frontal
attacks, either in war or politics, if there were a way round.'[1]
The way round in regard to Ireland was to invite the Irish
to find a solution for themselves, and the Convention of 1917
took the Irish question out of British politics while it lasted.
Even when the Convention failed, the blame could be laid on
the Irish, not on Lloyd George. The rise of Sinn Fein, too,
played into his hands. The Nationalists, discredited by Sinn
Fein victories at by-elections, virtually seceded from the
house and so finally parted from Asquith. Lloyd George
could denounce Sinn Fein as subversive: 'They are organizing
for separation, for secession, and for Sovereign independence. . . . Under no conditions can this country possibly
permit anything of that kind.'[2] This absolved him from
blaming Ulster in any way, which would have offended the
Unionists; while the Coalition Liberals abandoned the Irish
cause in outraged patriotism.

The Irish question raised a final complication in the spring
of 1918. The German offensive which began on 21 March
marked a moment of supreme crisis. It provoked a cry for
something dramatic even though irrelevant. As in 1916, the
dramatic act was conscription—this time the raising of the
age to 50. The Unionists threw in the demand that conscription be extended to Ireland. Perhaps they did this to embarrass their Liberal associates. More probably it was merely
another illustration of the general rule in British history that

---

[1] Lloyd George, *War Memoirs*, iv. 2274.
[2] 23 October 1917; *Hansard*, 5th series, xcviii. 790.

even the most reasonable men take leave of their senses as soon as they touch the Irish question. At any rate the proposal offered Asquith positively his last opportunity: he could rally the Liberals, and even the Nationalists, against Irish conscription and for Home Rule. But this was the very moment when Asquith was hoping to champion the military leaders (who also, of course, favoured Irish conscription) with Carson as his ally; hence he remained silent. Lloyd George worked out an ingenious compromise by which the Irish should get Home Rule and conscription together. In fact, they got neither, and Lloyd George covered the muddle by detecting a German plot in Ireland—one of those far-fetched stories which a British government produces when all else fails. In June 1918 this story served to tide things over until the end of the war. The Irish question never threatened to lead the Coalition Liberals back to Asquith.

The House in fact disliked discussion of great issues. It stirred uneasily when anyone, even Lloyd George himself, attempted to survey the general course of the war. It was aggressively intolerant when anti-war members raised the question of peace terms, or strayed otherwise into foreign policy. For instance, when Joseph King tried to discuss British policy towards Bolshevik Russia, Lord Robert Cecil espied strangers and secured a secret session with general approval. There was nothing secret in the topic; the house simply did not want to discuss it, or indeed anything else connected with the war. This is not to say that members were idle or indifferent to public affairs. Away from high policy, they showed considerable competence and devotion. They worked hard on electoral reform, virtually without guidance from the government, and made Great Britain a genuine democracy for the first time: universal manhood suffrage, and limited women's suffrage into the bargain. They helped Fisher to revolutionise secondary education. But they would have nothing to do with the great questions of the war. They believed, rightly as it turned out, that the Opposition would be slaughtered at a general election. More important, the supporters of the Coalition were determined not to reveal their own internal differences. The unavowed compact of the front benches with which the war started became an equally unavowed compact of the back benches before the end. The backbenchers had no idea how Lloyd George would win the war; they often disapproved of his policy when they understood it. But they clung firmly to the belief that he was not one of the 'Old Gang' under whom they had groaned for the first two years of the war. This was Lloyd George's decisive asset, though also his final liability. He was enough of a 'rogue' to eclipse wilder demagogues like Pemberton Billing and Horatio Bottomley. But, not being one of the 'Old Gang', he was expendable. When the war was over, he was expended.

II

THE MAN IN THE CLOTH CAP

A VISITOR to the house of commons in 1892 would have seen an assemblage of great figures. Gladstone was prime minister, preparing for his last battle over Home Rule; his memories going back beyond Palmerston, beyond the repeal of the Corn Laws to the political world before the great Reform Bill. Harcourt, John Morley, Joseph Chamberlain were on the front benches; Haldane and Grey were showing their first distinction. A shrewd observer could have spotted four future prime ministers: Balfour, Campbell-Bannerman, Asquith, Lloyd George. Even the shrewdest would have spared a glance at the member for West Ham (South) only as the sensation of a day: the man in a cloth cap, whose supporters brought him down to Westminster in a two-horse brake with a trumpeter on the box. It seemed a vulgar demonstration. But the trumpet sounded the note of doom both for the Liberal party and for old privileged England.

The man in the cap was Keir Hardie; and though he then stood alone, the only 'unwhipped' member of the House, he was to do more for the shaping of the future than all the giants who surrounded him. The Labour party and the Welfare State were both his children. He made the political and social order in which we now live. No doubt some such outcome would have happened in any case; but not quite as or when it did.

Keir Hardie was that rare character, a truly independent working-man. Independence was the key-word of his career. 'I know what I believe to be the right thing, and I go and do it.' He lost his job as a miner for taking the lead against the

45

mine-owner. He founded the Independent Labour Party, and he was the principal agent in creating independent Labour representation in Parliament. Yet he was equally insistent in demanding freedom from his own colleagues. He ran his own paper, took his own line on the public platform. He wanted the Labour party to be a federal body, 'leaving each organization free to maintain and propagate its own theory in its own way', and he refused to be tied by instructions from a party conference. His political outlook stemmed neither from Marx nor from Methodism, but from Robert Burns. 'I owe more to Robert Burns than to any man dead or alive.'

Hardie's socialism has been called emotional. Certainly he hated poverty and oppression. He was more moved on 23 June 1894 by the death of 260 miners in a colliery disaster than by the birth of a royal baby. He was not ashamed to point the contrast between the luxury of the wealthy classes and the death of children by starvation. But this was a statement of fact, not a rhetorical flourish. Fundamentally Hardie started from the simple proposition that the only rational form of society was one which recognized 'the divine spark' in every man.

Faith in humanity gave Keir Hardie his power. He was not a great orator; what moved his audiences was 'the homely, essentially human tone'. His writing had a soggy romantic flavour which made it much inferior to Blatchford's. But he had a burning faith that carried all before it. Hardie believed unquestioningly in the virtue of the working class, and he believed that this virtue would lead to a Socialist order. The Labour party has always been torn between immediate social reforms and the ideal community of the future. Hardie saw no conflict of loyalties. They were two different aspects of 'the Cause': and it is this union for the Cause which maintains the Labour party to the present day.

Not that Hardie ever put material benefits first. Though he repudiated the class war, no man was more class-conscious or, rather, class-confident. He had no interest in going up in the world. 'Emancipation' meant for him that privilege should cease, not that the children of working-class families should have a share in these privileges. Bernard Shaw once called Hardie 'the damnedest natural aristocrat in the House of Commons'. In fact, Hardie was something beyond Shaw's comprehension: a natural democrat. Towards the end of his life he told the I.L.P.: 'Nature never intended me to be a leader. I find myself happier among the rank and file.'

Hardie assumed that every Socialist must be a Radical. This belief gave him strength; it also, perhaps, led him to misjudge the future of the Labour party. He never thought of himself as one of 'His Majesty's Opposition'. Rather he regarded all institutions, including Parliament, as 'quaint without being impressive'. Parliament was important to him as the instrument of democracy, not as the emblem of historic continuity. He wore his cloth cap without affectation. Later he dressed more as an artist, with a long cloak and flowing cravat. But it is inconceivable that he would ever have worn the robes of a Knight of the Garter. In 1908 he criticized Edward VII's visit to the tsar at Reval. The king retaliated by striking him off the list of guests at a royal garden party. The stroke miscarried. Keir Hardie had never attended a garden party, and at first did not know he had been excluded. When the news reached him, he said: 'If I am fit to represent the working classes of Merthyr, I am fit to attend the garden party at Windsor' and all the Labour M.P.s boycotted the garden party until the exclusion was lifted.

In his first stretch in Parliament, between 1892 and 1895, Keir Hardie stuck exclusively to social affairs and never opened his mouth on imperial or foreign questions. The Boer war broke his silence. He became an extreme pro-Boer, desiring not compromise but a Boer victory, and he dreamt of a great Radical party on an anti-imperialist basis. He even offered to put himself under the leadership of the individualist John Morley. Hardie's fraternity did not stop with the people of England. It embraced all the people in the world. He gave great offence by sympathising with the national movement in India, and he advised the nationalists of Egypt in their first, stumbling steps.

After 1906, when he had some forty Labour colleagues in parliament, he increasingly left social reform to others and preached international conciliation. He became a great figure in the Socialist International and was largely responsible for its resolution on the general strike against war. The German Socialists regarded this as a pious gesture; Hardie took it seriously. The outbreak of war broke his heart. What shattered him was not so much the war in itself as that the working class went along with it. He said after a rowdy meeting in Merthyr, his constituency: 'I understand what Christ suffered in Gethsemane as well as any man living.'

He died on 26 September 1915. On his death the political truce was broken; and Merthyr returned a bellicose trade unionist in his place. Now, too, any Labour party members eager to fight for N.A.T.O. must be relieved that Keir Hardie lies a-mouldering in his grave. Perhaps his soul goes marching on.

III

THE ANGLO-RUSSIAN ENTENTE

THE Anglo-Russian entente was formally concluded on 31 August 1907. Unlike the Entente Cordiale with France, it has vanished into the mists of history. Yet, for good or ill, it ranks high among the significant events of the century. Its making and its ten years of existence changed the face of the world. The Anglo-French entente, though sentimentally admirable, was no more than a renewal of good relations which had been temporarily interrupted by rivalry in the Nile valley. The entente with Russia was a revolution. Great Britain and Russia had never been on close terms before, at any rate not since the end of the Napoleonic wars. Usually, indeed, they had been on bad terms—at war in the Crimea, and on the brink of war over Pendjeh in 1885. Continental statesmen, especially German, based their plans on the expected clash between the elephant and the whale. Instead the two countries composed their differences, cooperated diplomatically, and finally, to their mutual surprise, found themselves partners in a great European war.

The agreement of 31 August was modest in form. The two Powers merely promised to keep their hands off the buffer states of Central Asia. Afghanistan and Tibet were to be left alone. Even in regard to Persia, which is often described as 'partitioned', the bargain was negative. The British were to keep out of the north, the Russians out of the south; the centre lay neutral between them. Sir Edward Grey boasted that, unlike some earlier agreements, this contained no secret clauses. He spoke the truth, yet there were understandings unwritten but binding.

The Russians received a hint that they would get concessions at the Straits if they behaved well for a few years. As a
matter of fact they had to wait until 1915 before they secured
the promise of Constantinople, and then they proved unable
to cash the cheque. More broadly, the two countries were
committed to diplomatic cooperation. The Triple Entente
came into existence, though both Grey and Izvolski tried to
avoid using the phrase. Neither side liked its implications.
The British had no wish to support Russia's ambitions in the
Balkans (so far as she had any); the Russians managed, more
successfully, to keep clear of the naval dispute between England and Germany. All the same, the consequences were
inescapable. Germany could no longer exploit her policy of
'the free hand', once England and Russia were on good terms.
Henceforward the Germans aimed to disrupt the Triple
Entente and when they failed flung themselves in exasperation against it.

The Anglo-Russian entente was a business deal, not a
matter of sentiment. In England it was unpopular as no
diplomatic step has been except the policy of 'appeasement'.
Most Conservatives swallowed it cynically as strengthening
the balance against Germany. Liberal ministers—Grey and
Morley, for example—excused it on the ground that otherwise large forces would have to be provided for the defence
of India. The Radical rank and file abhorred the friendship
with an autocratic Power, the more so when Russia's only
democratic Duma had been recently dissolved. In 1908 the
Labour party protested, with some Radical support, against
Edward VII's visit to the tsar at Reval; and their renewed
protests kept the tsar confined to Cowes when he wished to
visit England the following year. The betrayal of Persia made
them yet more indignant. English Radicals believed that
Persia could maintain her own independence of Russia if she
received some British backing, and they were probably right.
It was additionally tiresome that, whatever the professions of
the Russian ministers at St. Petersburg—and they were perhaps sincere—the representative at Tehran went cheerfully
on encroaching as he had done for years. Persia caused Grey

more trouble than any other question in foreign affairs. Exasperation with Russian behaviour made him threaten to resign and to make way for a pro-German foreign secretary —a step that would have been welcome to the Liberal majority in the House.

At the outset the Radical critics complained that Persia had been sacrificed to 'that foul idol, the Balance of Power'; it had been the price for Russian backing against Germany. Later they turned the accusation the other way round and made out that the peace of Europe was being endangered for the sake of Imperialist gains in Persia and elsewhere. These charges were too simple. The entente was a bargain of mutual advantage; and, if this weakened Germany's position, Great Powers cannot be expected to bicker merely to please some third party.

The real British commitment was to France, not to Russia; but undoubtedly Great Britain had to be somewhat complaisant towards Russia in order to ensure that France could count firmly on her eastern ally. The British government decided, rightly or wrongly, not to tolerate a German hegemony of the Continent. Once having decided this, they had to go along with Russia in the last resort. In peacetime Russia benefited more than Great Britain from the entente. When war came it was the other way round. It was the Russian army which ensured that there should be a Western front in the first World war and which, moreover, ensured that the Germans could never put their whole weight on that front until too late.

In Russia, too, the policy of the entente was not without its critics, though occupying almost exactly reverse positions from those in England. The Russian liberals wanted to turn towards Europe and away from Asia. Therefore they welcomed the compromise over imperial interests and, still more, friendship with the Western Powers. The realists of the extreme Right deplored being involved in European affairs; and, paradoxically, Lenin shared their view. Lenin and Witte both regarded the entente as the root of all evil. Both wanted the European Powers to destroy themselves in a great war, while Russia developed the riches of her Asiatic empire.

The first Russian revolution of March 1917 would have marked the triumph of the entente, if it had been a triumph for anything. The Bolshevik revolution ended the entente and led logically not only to the peace of Brest-Litovsk but to the Nazi-Soviet pact. The Anglo-Russian entente has been forgotten by both partners. Yet, oddly enough, it has been more successful than the Anglo-French entente as a practical arrangement. England is no longer paramount in Egypt, nor France in Morocco. But the buffer states of Asia survive. Tibet is safe from Russia or the British Empire. Afghanistan is still neutral and independent. Most remarkable of all, Persia still defies Imperialist encroachment from every quarter with supreme self-confidence.

IV

'WE WANT EIGHT, AND
WE WON'T WAIT'

ARMAMENT programmes have often been the subject of controversy in British politics from the 'French panic' of 1860 to nuclear weapons at the present day. No controversy has been fiercer than that over naval building in March 1909. The phrase then coined still rings down the avenues of time. 'We want eight, and we won't wait.' The Liberal party, with its great majority, was deeply divided on this question; the cabinet itself threatened to disintegrate. The Unionists saw their chance to reverse the electoral defeat of 1906. They exploited popular passion, and believed office to be again within their grasp.

The origin of the crisis lay in 1906 when Sir John Fisher, first sea lord, introduced the Dreadnought, the first all-big-gun ship. The Dreadnought made all existing navies out of date; it was more powerful than three of its immediate predecessors put together. For the time being the Dreadnought increased British superiority and upset all other programmes; the Germans did not lay down a single battleship for nearly two years. But the superiority, though greater, rested on a narrower margin. In March 1909 the British had 43 pre-Dreadnought battleships as against 22 German. They had two of Dreadnought type completed and three battlecruisers; the Germans had none. But the Germans had fourteen ships projected; the British only seven. The gap between the two navies might close ominously when the Germans began to build.

Here was the second and more dangerous point. It had

always been assumed that Great Britain, as the greatest industrial Power, could build more ships than any other Power and could build them faster. Even if another country stole a march on the British, they could catch up before the danger point was reached. Gladstone had said it in 1894: 'Our means of construction are overwhelming. . . . Our methods of construction are far more rapid.' Goschen, Unionist first lord, repeated this confidence in 1898. Ten years later it was ceasing to be true in the opinion of many experts. Germany, too, was now an industrial Power of the first rank. Though still inferior in the number of her shipyards, she was equal, if not ahead, in the armament factories producing the guns, gun-mountings, turrets, and armourplate which a battleship needed. The Germans could, if they put themselves to it, build up to the British programme; and, what was more, with their industrial efficiency, they could build as fast, if not faster.

It was the duty of the expert advisers to tell the government how British supremacy could be maintained. By 1909 they had reached the conclusion that the yardstick should no longer be German ships, built or projected, but German capacity. This opened the door to fantastic calculations. The needs of the German army were ignored; all budgetary considerations disregarded. The only question was: how many battleships can the Germans have if they concentrate on this and nothing else? According to the published programme, the Germans would have ten battleships completed in the spring of 1911. Asquith, the Prime Minister, striking a moderate note, held that they would have thirteen or at most seventeen. Balfour, Leader of the Opposition, excelled in these speculative subtleties; according to him, the Germans would have at least 21 battleships in 1911, but more probably 25.

In face of these imagined perils the board of admiralty wished to increase the British building programme for 1909 from four battleships to six, and to maintain this rate for the two years following. The Unionists, supported by the popular press, raged that eight should be laid down at once. Two members of the cabinet, Lloyd George and Winston Churchill, stood out against the clamour. They pointed to the published German figure of ten for March 1911; four British battleships a year, added to the existing number, would be adequate to meet this. Germany, they argued, was a constitutional country. Battleships could not be built without the financial authorization of the Reichstag. What evidence, they asked, was there that the German admiralty was cheating either the Reichstag or the British experts?

The question could be given a theoretical answer. Germany, it could be alleged, was not a constitutional country in the British sense. The Reichstag would forgive a breach of the rules—as the Prussian parliament had forgiven Bismarck in 1866—if it brought strategic gain; and of course the German government had no moral obligation towards Great Britain to observe its published programme, whatever it might have towards the Reichstag. But there was also a more practical answer. There was evidence that some of the contracts for the German 1909–10 programme had been given out in the autumn of 1908, and evidence too that material for the projected ships had been collected in advance.

This is the most puzzling part of the story. We do not know to this day why the Germans 'anticipated' their 1909 programme. It may have been to break the ring of contractors or to provide continuity of employment. To suspicious British eyes it looked like an attempt to steal a march. The information came from secret sources. It could not be used publicly. But Fisher saw to it that it did not stay with the Government; it reached, probably in exaggerated form, the leaders of the Opposition and the press. Thus there were two supposed dangers: the theoretical possibility of German 'acceleration', the actual probability of German 'anticipation'. The argument plunged into inextricable confusion—men hinting at the second when they were ostensibly talking of the first.

Asquith handled the crisis with his customary adroitness, apparently doing one thing with the intention later of being forced to do the other. In the debates of March 1909 he stood solid with Lloyd George, Churchill, and the bulk of Liberal M.P.s. There was, he insisted, no danger, no need for panic; the building programme would remain at four battleships. But he asked also for authorisation to lay down four 'contingent' ships later in the year, if this proved necessary. Both parties were satisfied. The Liberals thought that agitation had been defied; the Unionists found that their thunder had been stolen. In July McKenna, first lord of the admiralty, announced that the four contingent ships would be built. He made no reference to German acceleration or anticipation; his new excuse was that Germany's two allies, Austria-Hungary and Italy, were proposing to build four Dreadnoughts at some time in the future. Everyone knew the real 'contingency': the Liberals had just suffered resounding defeat in a by-election at Croydon.

Only 79 Liberals voted vainly against the contingent ships. Thus the British public got their eight ships and did not wait. But the panic did the Unionists no good. To meet the increased naval bill Lloyd George devised the People's Budget, and soon his Limehouse speech drowned the cry of 'We want eight'. As to the supposed danger period of spring 1911, the Germans did not then have 25 battleships or 21 or seventeen or thirteen; they had six. A year later they had nine, against the British sixteen. Had they ever planned to have more? The answer might be found in the German naval records which, for some years after the second World war, reposed at Admiralty House and maybe are there still. No curious eye has looked upon them. British admirals guard the secrets of their German colleagues as carefully as they guard their own; or perhaps, considering Fisher's constant leakages, rather better.

V

AGADIR: THE *PANTHER*'S SPRING

ON 1 July 1911 the German gunboat *Panther* arrived off
Agadir, a port closed to European shipping in southern
Morocco. Her ostensible purpose was to rescue endangered
Germans. There were no Germans at Agadir. The nearest
was at Mogador, many miles away. He arrived at Agadir
to be endangered only on 4 July, and he was duly rescued the
following day. The real German object was political: to
stake out a claim to territory, at Agadir or elsewhere, before
Morocco fell to pieces.

This dissolution was supposed to be imminent, though the
expectation has turned out wrong: Morocco is now independent and united. In the first years of the century old Morocco
was in a bad state, and the French seemed to be moving in.
German threats stayed this process in 1905; and a conference
at Algeçiras the following year affirmed the independence of
Morocco, though France and Spain were entrusted with the
police of certain ports. The old order went on crumbling,
assisted no doubt by the two policing Powers. In May 1911
French forces marched on Fez, the capital, again to rescue
Europeans mythically endangered, much as Jameson had
marched to the rescue of 'girls in the gold-reef city' of
Johannesburg in 1895. The French were thus tearing up the
Act of Algeçiras; and this time the Germans had some
legal standing to justify their intervention.

Kiderlen the German secretary of state, planned a double
stroke. By settling the question of Morocco, he would
improve relations between France and Germany, and thus
weaken the Anglo-French entente. At the same time, by

collecting the French Congo as compensation, he would prepare the way for a German empire in Africa, stretching from the Atlantic to the Indian Ocean. The *Panther* was sent to Agadir from the strange notion that strong action— 'Banging the table', Kiderlen called it—would make concession easier for the French.

Caillaux, the French premier, was eager to concede. Always the advocate of Franco-German cooperation, he, too, planned a double stroke. First Franco-German reconciliation over Morocco; then, with German backing, he would deny to Spain the share of Morocco which she had been promised in 1904 on British insistence. But it was harder for him to take this line when negotiating under threats. The *Panther's* spring wrecked the policy which it was designed to further.

The British government were in a quandary over Morocco. Official policy was to desire a settlement between France and Germany. Their conflict, it was often said, was the main cause of Anglo-German tension; remove it, and good relations between Great Britain and Germany would be restored. The permanent staff of the foreign office were not so sure. They wanted an 'independent' France, that is, one that would stand on the British side against Germany; logically, from their point of view, they regarded Caillaux as a 'traitor'. The arrival of the *Panther* played into their hands. They proposed to 'stand by France', though their assistance had not been asked for. The British Government should raise the bid. The British, in their turn, should send a warship to Agadir (a bigger one of course). Sir Edward Grey favoured this.

The Radical members of the cabinet, a majority, did not. They sympathised with the German case. Germany was entitled, like other European Powers, to her 'place in the sun'; more specifically, she was entitled to compensation if the Act of Algeçiras were destroyed. For that matter Great Britain was entitled to compensation also, in spite of the fact that in 1904 she had been compensated once already (by the French abandonment of their rights in Egypt). Thus, throughout July, as the Franco-German negotiations secretly proceeded, there were two British policies in the event of a breakdown: a foreign office policy of military and naval backing for France; a Radical policy of a new conference, at which France would have to pay a high price.

On 21 July Lloyd George resolved the dilemma. A few sentences in his speech at the Mansion House that evening satisfied both British policies. He did not take sides between France and Germany, as came to be believed later. He merely said that Great Britain could not be ignored when a great international question was being settled. This could be interpreted as support for France; it could also be interpreted as support for a conference directed against France. As always, Lloyd George knew how to keep his hands free for the future. Expert opinion read the speech as directed against France, or rather directed against the exclusive Franco-German deal which Caillaux favoured. Caillaux, not Kiderlen, was disconcerted by the Mansion House speech. The German press, however, took it as a challenge. Kiderlen found himself swept away in an unwelcome flood of bellicosity.

The British press responded. 'Agadir' became a crisis in Anglo-German relations, a test of strength between the two countries. The British navy was sent to its war stations. Practical plans for sending an expeditionary force to the aid of France were now first authorised; the navy, much to its anger, was forced to cooperate in them. Lloyd George, ingenious as ever, turned the crisis to practical use. By raising the shadow of war, he settled a national railway strike: he persuaded the companies to meet the union representatives, whom they had always refused to meet before, and to accept very largely the union's demands. Perhaps it was with this in view that he made the Mansion House speech in the first place.

Then the crisis fizzled out. Kiderlen and Caillaux reached agreement, as they had meant to do all along. Germany got two strips of French colonial territory which gave her access to the Congo; France got a protectorate over Morocco. Their larger hope was disappointed. Kiderlen was denounced in the Reichstag as a weakling, the crown prince ostentatiously applauding the speeches against him. Caillaux was similarly denounced in France. He was overthrown early the following year, and his place taken by assertive nationalists, the Government of the *réveil national*. The outstanding cause of Franco-German conflict had been removed; yet Franco-German reconciliation was farther off than before.

The result of negotiation was estrangement; on the other hand, the result of quarrel between Great Britain and Germany was reconciliation. 'Agadir' raised a storm in England against Sir Edward Grey. The dissident Radicals organized against him in the Foreign Policy Committee with R. C. K. Ensor as secretary; they were energetically supported by C. P. Scott and the *Manchester Guardian*. New, and more successful, attempts were made to improve Anglo-German relations: Haldane visited Berlin; every practical question was settled from the Bagdad railway to the future of the Portuguese colonies.

Agadir was not really the prelude to the first World war except in date. It was the last of the colonial disputes which had disturbed international relations for the preceding 25 years and all of which had been settled peacefully. But it established a myth that the basic causes of European tension were imperialist and extra-European. Men went on believing this even when a great war broke out over a purely East European issue and was fought purely for European objects. The ultimate gainers from the crisis of Agadir were E. D. Morel and the Union of Democratic Control; or, more remotely, Lenin, author of *Imperialism: the Last Stage of Capitalism*. As for Agadir, it became a flourishing resort, developed the largest sardine-canning factory in the world, and was then ravaged by an earthquake.

VI

THE SCHLIEFFEN PLAN

THE invasion of Belgium was the keystone of German strategy in 1914. It was meant to bring total victory, immediate and decisive. Instead it brought England into the war, and ended in defeat on the Marne. What went wrong? The plan had been designed by Schlieffen, German chief of staff from 1891 to 1906; and his admirers claimed that it contained the infallible 'secret of victory'. The younger Moltke, his successor, was accused of ruining the plan by strengthening the German left in Alsace and by detaching two army corps for the Russian front. He would have won the war, it was alleged, in six weeks if he had adhered strictly to Schlieffen's recipe. Moltke's failure and Schlieffen's wisdom have become a universal legend. But in all the discussion the Schlieffen plan was never published—only fragments and detached sentences.

Now we have the full text: Schlieffen's testament as written for his successor on 31 December 1905, and with it the earlier stages in his strategy.[1] Schlieffen's wisdom turns out to be a myth. Professor Ritter, who has edited the text with scrupulous scholarship and an historical commentary, writes: 'The plan was by no means a certain recipe for victory. It was a rash gamble, the success of which depended on many strokes of luck.' Schlieffen himself called it 'an undertaking for which we are too weak'.

The story is from first to last a warning against a strategy that thinks in purely military terms. The elder Moltke had won great victories: over Austria in 1866, over France in

[1] Gerhard Ritter, *Der Schlieffenplan.*

1870. After 1871 he recognized that these could not be repeated. Russia would not again stand idly by while Germany won new victories in the west. But Moltke did not complain. Germany, he believed, could defend herself successfully. Her western front was impregnable against a French attack. Therefore the bulk of his army could ward off Russian invasion in the east—as indeed happened in 1914 with a much smaller force than Moltke postulated. Germany would not conquer all Europe but Moltke had no desire to do so. His task was to make her secure; and this he could accomplish. His strategy coincided precisely with Bismarck's policy after 1871, which was also pacific and defensive.

Schlieffen rejected this outlook from the moment he entered office. He started from the dogma (quite incorrect as both World wars proved) that no great Power could conduct a modern war for more than a few weeks. Therefore he must provide an immediate and total victory over one of Germany's foes, so as to be able to turn with equal rapidity against the other. But Russia could not be thus beaten in a few weeks—she had too much space. Therefore the whole German army must be hurled against France. It is sometimes said that Schlieffen's strategy was dictated by the Franco-Russian alliance. This is not so. He was a pure technician with no interest in politics. His argument rested on geography and logistics, not on political alliances, and he would have reached exactly the same conclusions if the Franco-Russian alliance had not existed (as indeed it did not when he first reached them). The only political factor that influenced him was of a different kind. Like most Prussians he detested his Austrian ally; and a war in the west could be fought without considering her.

The decision to knock out France was the vital step in principle. But how was it to be accomplished? The French front on the Vosges was as impregnable as the German, and a few staff exercises convinced Schlieffen that a breakthrough was impossible. For a few years he dreamt that the French would 'oblige' him by taking the offensive themselves. Then they could be defeated in the open field. He soon abandoned this dream. In 1897 he took his next jump. He would turn the French front at Verdun by going through Luxembourg. At once new difficulties arose. The French could now attack the right flank of the German invaders. Moreover, if he could violate the neutrality of Luxembourg the French could do the same in Belgium and at one point Schlieffen almost persuaded himself that he must invade Belgium purely as a defensive measure. He soon gave this up —unlike other German apologists: and his case for going through Belgium was solely that he needed to do so. Each year he designed the swing on his right more widely— through Holland as well as through Belgium; to the Channel coast; finally to the west of Paris, leaving the city itself 'sealed off' with a reserve army of 150,000 men.

The operation seems wonderful when one looks at the great encircling arrows drawn by Schlieffen on the map. But it rested on a grotesque miscalculation. It assumed that German soldiers could get round the outside of a circle faster on their own two legs than the French Army could move along the radius of the circle by rail. Joffre nearly obscured this when he 'obliged' the Germans by launching a catastrophic offensive in Lorraine. Even so, he won the battle of the Marne; and if the Germans had carried out Schlieffen's last plan of going west of Paris their disaster would have been all the greater.

The Schlieffen plan was supposed to face the situation that Germany had two enemies and that she was inferior to them in numbers. In practice it was a plan for superior numbers in a one-front war. It assumed that Russia could be ignored— Schlieffen even suggested that it would do no harm if the Russians took Berlin. Its final draft was completed at the end of 1905, when Russia had almost ceased to exist as a Great Power, and is actually called 'War against France in alliance with England'. Moreover it made limitless demands on German manpower: one army to seal off Antwerp; another to guard lines of communications; a third to seal off Paris. Yet none of these armies existed, as Schlieffen admitted.

The younger Moltke took over this plan, apparently because

he could think of nothing better. He made one profound modification: he left out Holland. This made it essential to seize Liège by surprise almost before the war started. Hence the reckless haste of the German general staff in August 1914, which made diplomacy impossible. Professor Ritter describes the invasion of Belgium as 'the beginning of Germany's and Europe's misfortune'. He is right. It was a blow from which faith in Germany has never recovered. We must admire a German who recognizes this frankly. But would Professor Ritter have condemned the Schlieffen plan so sternly if it had succeeded?

A final point of special interest to Englishmen. Some Radicals argued in 1914 that we could have protected the neutrality of Belgium if we had not been committed to France. Professor Ritter has found the answer to this in a memorandum drawn up by the younger Moltke in 1913:

Should we renounce the march through Belgium, in case England promises neutrality? That would be very dangerous, for it is quite uncertain whether England would keep her promise; but we should give up the only chance of a quick and decisive victory, which we need. Only if England went with us, would a renunciation of the march through Belgium be possible. That however is inconceivable. . . .

Military needs determined policy, not the other way round.

VII

HOW A WORLD WAR BEGAN

(i) *Murder at Sarajevo*

ON 28 June 1914 Gavrilo Princip, a Bosnian Serb schoolboy
of nineteen, shot and killed the Archduke Franz Ferdinand,
heir to the Habsburg throne, at Sarajevo. Everyone knows
this just as he knows that the battle of Hastings was fought
in 1066 or the battle of Waterloo in 1815. What lay behind
it? How did the two men make their date with destiny—the
slight unknown schoolboy and the man who should have
ruled a great empire? What strange chances brought them
together in this little hillside town?

Sarajevo is not much of a place, only a long cluster of
houses alongside a turbulent mountain stream, the Miliachka. In one way it is unique. Though the inhabitants are
all of Slav stock—mostly Serbs—about a third of them are
Mohammedans. These are descended from Serb landowners
who changed their faith to save their lands, and perhaps their
Bogomil heresy, at the time of the Turkish conquest. For 400
years the Turks made Sarajevo the administrative capital of
Bosnia, so far as they did any administering.

Bosnia was always a trouble area. Elsewhere in Europe the
Turks ruled over helpless Christian peasants. In Bosnia they
were faced with independent landowners who, though
Mohammedan, remained arrogant and rebellious, just as
the Protestants of Ireland led the national movement there
until the beginning of the nineteenth century. Bosnia was the
scene of repeated revolts. The last of them, in 1875, touched

off the great Eastern crisis which ended three years later at the Congress of Berlin.

The Great Powers decided not to put Bosnia back under Turkish rule. There was a great Christian Power eager to take it over. The Habsburg Monarchy, which had acquired the name of Austria-Hungary in 1867, had lost its Italian lands and its hegemony in Germany; but it was still ostensibly a Great Power, still anxious to restore its prestige. To save appearances, the Congress preserved Turkish sovereignty, and handed over the administration of Bosnia to the Austrians.

They, too, had hard fighting before they established their authority. Then they built the monuments of their rule: a museum, a town hall, some cafés, and many barracks. In the 'Age of Imperialism', Bosnia became Austria-Hungary's substitute for colonies in Africa. Here, ethnographers, remittance-men, financiers, army officers, found a refuge or careers.

Turkish sovereignty remained a theoretical nuisance. In 1908 the Austrian statesmen decided to get rid of it. They annexed Bosnia. This caused an international crisis though no war. The technical outcome was a treaty by which Turkey surrendered Bosnia in exchange for financial compensation. This treaty was never ratified by the Austrian or Hungarian Parliaments. Austria-Hungary existed only for external affairs: it had an army and a foreign policy but no domestic existence. At home there were two separate states, Austria and Hungary. Bosnia, once formally acquired, must have b en incorporated in one or the other. But which? The question would have raised fierce, perhaps insoluble, dispute. Therefore Bosnia was left in suspended animation, still merely administered, owned by nobody. The Ottoman Empire had surrendered it; the Habsburg Monarchy had not completed the legal process for taking it over. Strictly speaking, Franz Ferdinand was on foreign soil when he came to Sarajevo on the sunny Sunday of 28 June 1914.

Why did he come? It is usually said that he came as a gesture of defiance against Serb nationalism; and certainly the Serbs began to look longingly towards Bosnia after the Balkan wars of 1912 and 1913 when they liberated Macedonia from the Turks. Bosnia was the next item on the agenda of national ambition. Yet this had little to do with it so far as Franz Ferdinand was concerned. It is not even clear whether he knew that he had chosen the Serb national day of St. Vitus, just as it is uncertain whether Hitler knew what anniversary he was celebrating when he fixed his attack on Russia for 22 June.

Franz Ferdinand was celebrating quite a different anniversary—his marriage to Sophie Chotek on 28 June 1900. For this stern man, stiff with pride, rigid to insanity on every trifle of etiquette and protocol, himself broke the strictest rule of the Imperial house: he married for love outside the permitted ranks of royalty. His wife was a mere countess; his marriage was morganatic; his children were disinherited. While the archduke as heir ranked immediately after the emperor, his wife came at the tail of every procession.

Franz Ferdinand loved deeply—it was his one redeeming feature. He wished to raise his wife to his own level; he would have made her empress if he had come to the throne, despite his vows of renunciation. He could not wait for his uncle's death. He wanted precedence for his wife here and now. And there was a way to get it.

Franz Ferdinand was Inspector-General of the Austro-Hungarian army, and on purely military occasions his wife too could enjoy her husband's supreme rank. Some place must be found where the civil authorities could be ignored and where the military ruled. This place was Bosnia: Potiorek, the Governor, a general, and the army on active service. The excuse was the annual army manœuvres. The real reason was that only in Bosnia could Sophie Chotek ride unchallenged by her husband's side.

This explains, too, a fact which has puzzled many writers: why the civil authorities were not consulted and why no precautions were taken. When the Emperor Franz Joseph visited Sarajevo, 200 political suspects were locked up for the day, and thousands of extra police drafted in. Now no one was in gaol; there were only 120 police for the whole town; and there was no attempt to line the archduke's route with soldiers. The civil authorities had expostulated some months before. They were told that the visit had nothing to do with them; naturally, therefore, they had nothing to do with the visit. As to the military authorities, they had always regarded the stories of unrest as political nonsense. Like most soldiers in occupied countries they hardly acknowledged that the local population existed except as cleaners in the barracks. It did not occur to the generals, nor even to Franz Ferdinand, that there would be any trouble at Sarajevo on 28 June, the day of St. Vitus.

The generals were very nearly right. Franz Ferdinand and his wife came to Ilidze, a little spa that served as military headquarters, on 25 June. He inspected troops, attended the manœuvres, visited the museum at Sarajevo and had a drink at the principal hotel. His wife was received everywhere with full honours, especially from young officers who had their careers to make. The Imperial pair were cheered whenever they appeared. Everything promised well for the formal visit to Sarajevo on Sunday morning. And everything would have gone well had it not been for a youth of nineteen who had left school four weeks previously.

Gavrilo Princip was a true 'student' of the period when the word covered anything from a schoolboy to an 'eternal student' in his forties. In France he would have rioted for, or against, the *Sacre du Printemps*. In Russia he would have been a Social Revolutionary. Being Bosnian, he was a Serb nationalist. He was a character from a Chekhov play except that when he fired he did not miss—much to his own surprise. This unexpected success made him the first of the countless young idealists who died for their country in the first World war. Not, of course, that he stood alone. All the educated youngsters of Bosnia talked sedition and conspiracy, particularly after Serbia's victories in the Balkan wars.

Princip got some of his grammar-school education in Sarajevo; some of it in Belgrade, the capital of Serbia. This bewilders us; a boy continuing his education with official sanction in the capital of a country which was plotting the ruin of his own. But so it was in those enlightened days. In Belgrade Princip and some of his school friends encountered a member of the Black Hand, and perhaps enrolled in that secret society.

The Black Hand had a name of terror, though—like most revolutionary societies—its practical achievement was small. Its members were mostly officers in the Serb army. Some of them had been involved in the murder of King Alexander Obrenovich in 1903. Since then they had talked a great deal about revolutionary conspiracies in Macedonia against the Turks. They had done nothing. Instead, Macedonia was liberated by open war. After the war army officers, claiming to represent the Black Hand, swarmed into Macedonia; offended the local population; lined their own pockets. Pasich, prime minister of Serbia, had tolerated the Black Hand when it had promised to be useful against the Turks. Now he was anxious to conciliate the inhabitants of Macedonia. Early in 1914 Pasich ended military rule in Macedonia and installed civil officials. The Black Hand was furious. Its secret powers, ineffective against the Turks, were turned against Pasich.

'Apis', the leader of the Black Hand, was in real life Colonel Dimitrievich, head of the Serbian Military Intelligence. Everyone in Belgrade knew his dual identity—a breach of security not unusual. Dimitrievich was an old friend of King Peter and had long been patronized by the Russian legation. He appealed to his backers and, with their aid, engineered Pasich's dismissal.

Then things went wrong for 'Apis'. King Peter was a sick man, weary of public life. He withdrew, leaving Crown Prince Alexander as Regent, and Alexander was an enemy of the Black Hand.

Perhaps even more important, Hartwig, the Russian Minister at Belgrade, changed sides. He had helped Serbia to launch the Balkan wars. Now he was warned from St. Petersburg that Russia did not want new trouble in the Balkans. Hartwig seconded the Regent's breach with the Black Hand. Pasich came back to office in triumph, determined to challenge the Black Hand and its sympathizers in the Serb parliament.

During these days of political conflict Princip and other Bosnian students were drifting round Belgrade, eager for some great stroke. Their own idea was to assassinate the block-headed Governor of Bosnia, General Potiorek. Their contact-man with the Black Hand offered an alternative: they should have a try at Franz Ferdinand instead. This is the one piece of independent evidence involving Dimitrievich and the Black Hand in the plot at all. For the archduke's visit had not yet been announced in the newspapers (where Princip claimed to have learnt of it); but it was known to the Serb Intelligence —that is, to Colonel Dimitrievich.

Assuming that the attempt was his suggestion, why did he suggest it? Was it, as he alleged later, to disrupt an Austro-Hungarian invasion of Serbia which was to follow the Bosnian manœuvres? Or, as some ingenious historians have hinted, to eliminate the Habsburg who might 'solve' the South Slav question? Neither of these. Dimitrievich was struggling for power in Belgrade, not pursuing nationalist ambitions in Bosnia. He was aiming at Pasich, not at Franz Ferdinand. Dimitrievich wanted a scandal, not a murder.

It never crossed his mind that these schoolboys might succeed. After all, none of his plans ever succeeded. But any disturbance in the streets of Sarajevo would be good enough. Consider what would follow. The Austro-Hungarian government would complain to Belgrade (as indeed they did). Then what would Pasich do? If he went against the conspirators and the Black Hand, he would be discredited in Serbia as an Austrian tool. If he defied the Austrians he would need the support of Dimitrievich and his secret society. Either way, Pasich would lose, and 'Apis' would win. The plot at Sarajevo was a move in Serb domestic politics.

This is the key to many mysteries. It explains why the conspirators received so little training. Princip, for instance, fired a few practice rounds from a revolver and missed the target. It explains why so little care was taken to cover the tracks of the conspirators into Bosnia. The threads were meant to lead back to Belgrade. It explains why the phials of poison, given to the conspirators, proved innocuous. These wretched boys were meant to fall into the hands of the Austro-Hungarian police.

It also explains on the other side the curious affair of the Serb warning in Vienna. For there were government agents in the Black Hand just as there were members of the Black Hand in government service. One of them tipped Pasich off. What to do? Arresting the conspirators would play Dimitrievich's game. Pasich therefore sent an obscure warning to Bilinski, the Austro-Hungarian minister of finance, who was in charge of Bosnia's administration. The warning reached the wrong man.

Bilinski was head only of the civil administration. He had not been consulted about the archduke's visit; and was now too proud to pass on the warning—not that Franz Ferdinand would have taken any notice if he had. Pasich took a final precaution. On 24 June he dissolved the Serbian parliament in the hope that a general election would give his people something else to think about as the bombs went off.

So the stage was set for 28 June—the schoolboy and the archduke moving on different paths to their date with destiny. The only considerable street in Sarajevo is the quay which runs alongside the River Miliachka. Here would pass the procession of four open cars, the archduke and his wife in the second of them. Here six youngsters were stationed by a pupil-teacher of twenty-four, named Ilich, who claimed to organize the attempt. There were no soldiers and few police. But the conspirators had forgotten that the cars would be moving. All their practice had been against stationary targets. They had overlooked, too, the crowds and the excitements.

As the cars came along and the cheers rolled, one conspirator—a printer of nineteen called Chabrinovich—knocked the detonator off his bomb. The detonator, flying wide, bruised Sophie Chotek in the neck. The bomb fell short. It exploded near the third car, damaging a wheel and injuring an officer.

The car was pushed on to the sidewalk; the procession, reduced to three cars, went on.

Of the other conspirators, one was so jammed in the crowd that he could not pull the bomb out of his pocket. A second saw a policeman standing near him and decided that any movement was too risky. A third felt sorry for the archduke's wife and did nothing. A fourth lost his nerve and slipped off home. Princip, the last of them, thought the plot had succeeded when he heard the explosion of the bomb. He began to push through the crowd with the intention of shooting Chabrinovich so as to prevent his talking. At that moment the cars went by with the archduke unharmed. Princip decided on suicide, but again without acting. He crossed the road glumly to a café, where he sat at a table and ordered coffee.

The 'death-ride' seemed safely over. Franz Ferdinand arrived at the town hall angry, not frightened; angry at this upset to the celebration of his wedding anniversary. He brushed aside the mayor's address of welcome. Sarajevo must be punished for its behaviour. He would withdraw his Imperial presence from it without delay. Instead of turning off the quay on his return journey for a tour of the old town, he would drive straight along the quay and away. The party climbed back into the cars.

There was no attempt at precaution except that Count Harrach, who had lent his car to the archduke for the day, stood on the running-board to ward off any further bombs from the riverside. Such was the bustle that the chauffeurs were not told about the change of plan. The driver of the first car turned into the old town, and the archduke's driver followed him. Potiorek called out: 'Not that way, you fool.' The driver stopped and laboriously backed into the quay with much grinding of gears.

At this moment Princip, sipping a glass of water after his coffee in the Austrian fashion, looked up and saw the archduke stationary before him not two yards away. He pushed out of the café, stepped on to the running-board of the car and shot Franz Ferdinand at point-blank range. He then aimed at Potiorek, who was sitting in the front seat, and hit the archduke's wife, who was sitting at the back. She died almost at once. Franz Ferdinand called out: 'Sophie, Sophie. Don't die. Live for the children.' He muttered half a dozen times: 'It is nothing', then fell back also and was dead before he could be lifted from the car. Such was the crime of Sarajevo.

The fate of the individual actors was soon eclipsed by the World war. It is worth an epilogue. The bodies of the Archduke and his wife were brought back to Vienna in botched obscurity. It would never do to pay Sophie Chotek Imperial honours. One coffin carried the full regalia of an archduke; the other, white gloves and a fan—symbol of Sophie's origin as a lady in waiting. There was none of the elaborate Habsburg ritual. The bodies were hurried away to a memorial chapel on the archduke's private estate. Franz Joseph, the emperor, commented: 'A higher Power has restored the order which I was unable to maintain.' He meant by this that Charles, the new heir-apparent, had married within the permitted degrees.

One of the conspirators escaped to Montenegro. Years later he returned to Sarajevo and ran a market garden. All the others were arrested and tried. Only Ilich was of age and therefore alone liable to the death penalty by Austrian law. He was duly hanged after attempting to turn king's evidence. The others were sentenced to long terms of imprisonment. Chabrinovich, Princip, and one other died in prison, more from hunger and damp than ill-treatment. The remaining two were released on the collapse of the Habsburg Empire. One of them became curator of the museum at Sarajevo; the other Professor of History at Belgrade University. They never spoke much of their historic moment, though not ashamed of it. Princip alone received the name of Hero.

Dimitrievich continued to serve as head of Military Intelligence, his feud with Pasich apparently forgotten on the outbreak of war. He made the winter retreat across the mountains to Corfu in 1915; and accompanied the Serb army to Salonika. There he was arrested in December 1916, and

c*

accused, along with other army officers, of attempting to
murder the Regent, Prince Alexander. The only serious
witness against him was a man already in prison for a
common murder. All the accused were found guilty. The
British and French governments protested against the trial.
Their protests were ignored, and Dimitrievich was shot,
along with two others, on 26 June 1917.

Shortly before his death he claimed that he had saved the
lives of most of his fellow-accused by threatening to reveal
the secrets of the Sarajevo affair. He is also said to have left
a confession that he organized the plot. The confession has
never been seen. Pasich had certainly had his revenge. But
why? Merely to eliminate a dangerous enemy? Or was it that
Pasich and Alexander were hoping to make a compromise
peace with Austria-Hungary in the spring of 1917 and offered
up Dimitrievich as a sacrifice? We shall never know.

Nor was the mystery ended. In 1953 the survivors of the
Salonika trial, now old men, were brought out of retirement
by the Communist government of Yugoslavia. The trial was
solemnly 'revised'. All the accused, including Dimitrievich,
were declared innocent. Again why? It was suggested that it
was to discredit the royal house among its remaining
adherents at home and in America. But few reports of the
trial were issued; and the English version, once promised,
was never released. Colonel Dimitrievich, the mysterious
'Apis', remained a man of mystery. Perhaps he had helped
to cause a world war. But a marriage for love had played its
part too.

(ii) *A Dead Man's Battle Orders*

July 1914 has produced more books than any other month
in modern history. Yet, to adapt a sentence from Sir Lewis
Namier in a different context: there would not be a great
deal to say on this subject were it not for the nonsense that
has been written about it.

Most of the nonsense has sprung from the very human
conviction that great events have great causes. The first

World war was certainly a great event. Therefore great causes have had to be found for it. Some have discovered a long-planned German design for conquering the world. Others have emphasized deep economic rivalries. Russia's ambition for Constantinople; German projects for a railway to Bagdad; the struggle between Teuton and Slav, or between despotism and democracy; all have been recited. To little purpose.

The truth is that the statesmen of Europe behaved in July 1914 just as they had behaved for the preceding thirty years, neither better nor worse. The techniques and systems which had given Europe a generation of peace now plunged her into war.

Two precise alliances gave a firm pattern to the relations of the Great Powers. Germany and Austria-Hungary were mutually pledged to resist an attack from Russia. France and Russia were pledged to resist an attack from Germany. Examined more closely, the pattern dissolves. The Powers had a tangle of interests and ambitions which cut across their formal commitments. The partners had not stood shoulder to shoulder over the years. Germany had often restrained Austria-Hungary from provoking Russia. France had often held Russia back from challenging Germany. No restraining voice was heard in July 1914.

The statesmen of Europe, with one accord, accepted the theory of 'the deterrent': the more strongly and firmly they threatened, the more likely they were both to preserve the peace of Europe and to get their way. The alliances had little to do with it, and none of the carefully defined pledges was evoked in the crisis of 1914. Germany attacked Russia before Austria-Hungary was threatened; France was attacked by Germany before she had decided whether to aid Russia.

None of the statesmen wanted war on a grand scale, but they wanted to threaten and they wanted to win. The peaceful outcome of previous crises increased the temptation to shout and bully. On the news of the assassination at Sarajevo, Berchtold, the Austro-Hungarian foreign minister, resolved that this time action, dramatic and decisive, must be taken against Serbia. He had protested often enough to Belgrade;

he had threatened. Now he must go beyond protests and threats to—what? It would be pointless to invade Serbia without annexing some of her territory, and equally pointless to add more discontented South Slavs to the Monarchy. Still, action there must be. First Berchtold wondered what to do; then he wondered whether to do it. Finally he relapsed into consulting his great German ally.

On 5 July a special emissary from Vienna arrived at Potsdam for lunch. William II started by being constitutionally correct: he could give no advice to Austria-Hungary, he said, without consulting the chancellor, Bethmann Hollweg. As lunch proceeded, he grew more excited. When it was over, he made his pronouncement. Austria should act at once; she should march into Serbia; and Germany would stand by her 'even if it came to a war between Austria-Hungary and Russia'.

Later in the afternoon Bethmann came to Potsdam. He went for a walk in the park with William II; heard the advice that had been given; and endorsed it. Austria-Hungary received a blank cheque; and, something more, was told to cash it at once. This was, as things turned out, the fatal decision which produced a great war. Yet William II and Bethmann did not intend it like that. They were merely clattering the sword as it had been so often clattered before.

Their strongest motive was to stiffen Austrian morale. For years Austria-Hungary had been going downhill. Jagow, the German secretary of state, remarked: 'Now she scarcely counts as a full-sized Great Power.' Indeed the Germans had almost reached the point of abandoning Austria-Hungary for some other ally. Only inability to decide between Russia and England held them back. If Austria at last acted, at last did something, this would pull her together; she would cease to be the Sick Man of Europe. Yet the Germans—William, Bethmann and the rest—only half-believed that Austria would act. Hence their lighthearted promises of support: they at least could not be blamed if Austria-Hungary again did nothing.

Moreover, the German rulers were firmly wedded to the

theory of the deterrent. A resolve to go to war, loudly proclaimed, and the other side would give way. In Jagow's words: 'The more boldness Austria displays, the more strongly we support her, the more likely Russia is to keep quiet.' Those who condemn the German policy should reflect that Sir Edward Grey did the opposite from the Germans: he failed to make his position clear in advance. And for this he has often been saddled with responsibility for the war.

However, general war seemed hypothetical and remote on 5 July. The irremediable blunder of the Germans was to assume that the affair would soon be settled one way or the other: either Austria-Hungary would act, or she would not. Everyone in Europe would have understood, and most would have sympathized, if the Austrians had struck against Serbia in immediate resentment.

Here the rigidity of mobilization plans first intervened with fatal effect. Swift action was impossible for the Habsburg army; indeed its attack on Serbia (which technically caused all the trouble) got under way only many weeks after the Powers of Europe were locked in conflict. Further, the Austrians were hoping to discover some evidence that the Serbian government had been involved in the crime— though they never did. In addition, President Poincaré was visiting St. Petersburg, and Berchtold wished to postpone the crisis till this visit was over.

Deep down these were all pretexts. The Austrians, as one of them wrote later, were like 'someone who is to undergo an operation and hopes more or less confidently to be able to escape it'. The Austrian ministers dithered on for more than a fortnight, so alarmed at their own intentions that they met in secret—the Ministers coming on foot to Berchtold's private house. By the time that the ultimatum was ready, most people had forgotten about Franz Ferdinand and Princip. Indignation, Austria-Hungary's one asset, had evaporated.

The ultimatum was presented in Belgrade on 23 July. It had been shown to the German statesmen beforehand;

contrary to their statements after the war, they made no
complaint against it. The Austrian government made no
attempt to discriminate between the Serb government and
the Black Hand. Perhaps they did not realize the bitter
internal conflict here. In any case their object was to humiliate
Serbia, not to exact reparation. Yet the Austrians could have
won Russian backing if they had concentrated against the
Black Hand.

Hartwig, the Minister at Belgrade, decided Russian policy.
Once the patron of the Black Hand, he had now turned against
it. On 10 July he came to the Austrian Legation, meaning to
propose Russian and Austro-Hungarian cooperation with
Prime Minister Pasich against the secret societies. Hartwig
was fat; he was excited; he was about to reverse Russian
policy. The strain was too much for him. As he reached the
critical sentence, his heart gave out. He slithered from his
chair on to the carpet, dead. The Russian government had
lost its one moderating influence.

Pasich had lost it too. Even so, his original intention was
to accept the Austro-Hungarian ultimatum without reserve.
He knew that the Serbian army was exhausted and unfit for
another war; he was doubtful of Russian backing. Characteristically, he planned to shift the responsibility on to his
colleagues. He left Belgrade on an election campaign; and
then slipped off to Salonika 'for a short holiday'. A peremp-
tory message from the prince regent caught him just before
his train crossed the frontier. Gloomily he returned to
Belgrade. However, he stuck to his decision: there must be
unconditional acceptance.

By the morning of 25 July, the Serbian reply was ready; it
accepted all the Austrian demands and removed any pretext
for war. Then the Serbian ministers changed round. The
draft was hacked to pieces: reservation changed to rejection,
new reservations introduced. Further changes were made in
ink on the final copy, the last of them only ten minutes
before the note was due for delivery.

What caused the change? Here is one of the few remaining
mysteries about July 1914 which documents still unpublished

—Serb documents—might explain. The accepted guess is that a promise of Russian backing had arrived from St. Petersburg; what is more, there came with it urgent advice that the Serbs should accept only part of the Austrian ultimatum. This was the second fatal decision, the counterpart of the promises to Austria-Hungary made by William II and Bethmann at Potsdam on 5 July.[1]

Yet the Russian government, too, did not want war. The Russian army was being remodelled; this reconstruction would not be complete until 1917. Of course Nicholas II and Sazonov, his Foreign Minister, had been invigorated by the stir and emotion of President Poincare's visit, but there is no evidence that the Austro-Serb crisis was discussed at all seriously. In the French agenda for the visit the topic of the archduke's murder came fourteenth on the list, and Poincare was more concerned to improve relations between England and Russia than to plan a European war.

If the visit had any importance for the crisis, it was to distract Sazonov's attention so that he could only make a decision at the last moment. Even then his decision was a decision not to decide. In urging the Serbs to give only a modified acceptance, he was, he supposed, holding the door open to further negotiation. The Austrians would renew their

[1] An alternative guess was suggested to me years ago by my master, Professor A. F. Přibram. According to him, the Russian government sent neither advice nor encouragement. The advice to accept the Austro-Hungarian note only with reservations was given to the Serbs by Berthelot, political director at the French foreign ministry, who was conducting foreign policy during the absence of Poincaré and Viviani in Russia. If this guess be correct, what was Berthelot's motive? To keep the question a-boil until the return of his official superiors? To prevent a reconciliation between Russia and Austria-Hungary at Serbia's expense? Perhaps, pushed on by French armament manufacturers, to ensure more orders from Serbia of French rifles and guns? Or merely the itch of a professional diplomatist to amend any draft submitted to him? Of course the Serbian government may have received advice from no one, and have amended the draft themselves at the last minute, either from fear of the Black Hand or to create a stir at the general election. In any case, it made no difference. The Austro-Hungarian government meant to step up their demands if the first lot were accepted, until a breaking-point was reached. Once statesmen take leave of their senses, they rarely get back to solid ground.

demands; Russia would urge a little more acceptance; and thus an honourable compromise would be reached.

Moreover, Sazonov had the bright idea that Russia could improve her bargaining position by a partial mobilization directed against Austria-Hungary alone. This would not threaten Germany; hence there would be no danger of general war. Here is the key to Sazonov's policy from 24 to 28 July: he thought that he could talk war without meaning it. There was a tiny flicker of sense in Sazonov's policy, more, indeed, than he knew. The Austrian army could crush Serbia only by deploying its whole strength.

The campaign of November 1914, when the Austrians were defeated and expelled from Serbia, shows this. The Austrians would be helpless if they had to station half their forces in Galicia. Failing a Russian promise of unconditional neutrality, they would have to do this in any case. Therefore Russia's partial mobilization had no real purpose.

It had, however, a fatal flaw on the other side. There were no prepared plans for mobilizing against Austria-Hungary alone. If these were now improvised and carried out, general mobilization would be impossible; Russia would be at Germany's mercy. Sazonov had devised a plan to hamstring Austria without noticing that it would also hamstring Russia. If he had been asked on 24 July: general war or nothing? he might well have answered: nothing. Instead, by projecting a little war, he made a great war inevitable.

The amateur strategist, devising actions without inquiring whether they were technically possible, was a recurring theme in July 1914. First Berchtold did it, now Sazonov; later Bethmann and finally Grey were to land in the same contradiction. It was no doubt the penalty for forty years of peace, years in which armies and campaigns had been weapons of diplomacy, not of war.

At five minutes to six on the afternoon of 25 July Pasich in person delivered the Serbian reply to the Austrian legation. The Austrian Minister glanced through the note; saw that it was not an unconditional acceptance; and, breaking off relations, left Serbian soil within the hour. The Austrian

spirit of resolution was now exhausted. Berchtold, once so
eager for action, went round telling everyone: 'Breaking off
relations does not necessarily mean war'; and he was
delighted to learn from Conrad, the chief of staff, that the
Austrian army could do nothing for at least a fortnight.

This behaviour did not meet with German approval.
Bethmann had hit on a policy which was to solve all
problems: the conflict was to be 'localized'. Austria-Hungary
would acquire prestige by crushing Serbia; and Germany
would get the credit for averting a European war. For the conflict to be localized, it had first to start. The Germans began
to push against Berchtold harder and harder, and he, in his
usual agreeable way, gave in to them.

On 28 July Austria-Hungary declared war against Serbia;
and therewith Berchtold saddled himself for ever with the
technical responsibility for starting the first World war.
Yet this was rather hard on him. The declaration of war was
not meant as a warlike action, merely as another measure of
diplomacy: its only purpose was to ensure that the Austro-
Serb dispute was not settled by compromise before it started.

In the next couple of days many diplomatists—principally
the British—devised a new way out: the Halt in Belgrade.
The Austrians should occupy Belgrade as a pledge, and then
stop. The idea might have worked. It broke down on an unexpected obstacle: the Austrians were incapable of occupying
Belgrade, even though the town was undefended.

Sazonov, too, favoured the Halt in Belgrade. But, for the
Austrians to stop, they must be warned by Russia. Talk was
not enough. Russia must act. Now was the moment for partial mobilization. But on 29 July Sazonov first learnt two
appalling facts. First, the Russian generals at last explained
to him that, if Russia partially mobilized against Austria-
Hungary, she would thereafter be unable to mobilize against
Germany. Secondly, the Germans, who had been as ill-
informed as Sazonov, changed round. As late as 28 July
Jagow had said: 'Russia's partial mobilization would not be
a reason for Germany to mobilize.'

On 29 July the German ambassador delivered a warning

that partial mobilization would provoke German mobilization—and war. Sazonov believed the first part of the warning;
he ignored the second. Having had partial mobilization in
his mind for days, he could not contemplate doing nothing.
The choice seemed to be: partial mobilization which would
leave Russia helpless against Germany and would yet provoke
her mobilization; or general mobilization which would also
cause Germany to mobilize but would enable Russia to
defend herself.

The answer seemed clear. Yet Sazonov still hesitated, and
the tsar yet more. On 29 July orders were drafted for both
partial and general mobilization. At 9 p.m. the tsar agreed
to general mobilization. At 9.30 he changed his mind; the
orders were cancelled. The following afternoon Sazonov and
a representative of the general staff saw the tsar again. The
general said: 'It is hard to decide.' Nicholas answered
roughly: 'I will decide', and signed the order for general
mobilization. Later he noted in his diary: 'I went for a walk
by myself. The weather was hot. Had a delightful bathe in
the sea.'

This time there was no going back. Russia's mobilization
began. Yet it was not a decision for war, only to put increased
diplomatic pressure on Austria-Hungary. The Austrian mobilization which followed on 31 July was a reply in kind: the
Austrians could not be ready for weeks. It was different in
Berlin. Here lay the essential factor which turned the July
crisis into a great war.

The Germans had no plans for mobilization; only a plan
for war. Others could call men to the colours; the Germans
could only march. The Germans wanted victory, not defence,
and for twenty years the general staff, under Schlieffen's
guidance, had pursued the mirage of winning a two-front war
with one army. The Germans were to march through Belgium
and destroy the French army before Russia was ready.

This was the essence of the Schlieffen Plan. Events
showed it to be wrong on every count. It was wrong in
asserting that Germany could not stand on the defensive
against France; she did so successfully on the Vosges only a

few weeks later. It was wrong in denying that the Germans could defeat Russia if there were also a western front; she did so by 1917 despite the British and French armies. It was wrong most of all in claiming that France could be annihilated by a march through Belgium; instead the Germans marched to defeat on the Marne. Absurdly enough, Schlieffen himself foresaw failure. He called his own plan 'an undertaking that is beyond our strength'.

Nevertheless, the Schlieffen Plan caused the outbreak of war. On 31 July Moltke, chief of the general staff, insisted that the last moment had arrived. The following dialogue decided the fate of Europe:

Bethmann: 'Is the Fatherland in danger?'

Moltke: 'Yes.'

Bethmann: 'Then we have no choice.'

At 1 p.m. the German plans began to operate. From that hour nothing could avert the outbreak of war. There remained only a formality to observe: the German ultimatums to France and Russia. They were drafted so as to ensure rejection. The Russians were asked not to proceed to general mobilization, although the Germans knew that they had already done so. Hence rejection was certain, and the Germans could declare war on 1 August.

The case of France was more difficult. Here the Germans had no conceivable grievance or complaint. They intended to demand from France a promise of neutrality; if this had been given they would have gone on to demand the surrender of Toul and Verdun. Viviani cut the discussion short; 'France would act according to her own interests.' The Germans did not renew their demand. It crossed their minds that, if France agreed to it, all their war plans would be ruined. Instead they invented the story that French aeroplanes had bombed Nuremberg. With this pretext Germany declared war against France on 3 August. Thus the armies rolled forward at the behest of a dead man, Schlieffen, who had never held command in any fighting of a serious character.

The most striking feature of the July crisis was the total lack of contact in every country between the political and military leaders. Military plans were at their most rigid in the railway age; yet no statesman had the slightest idea what the timetables involved. Their sensations, when diplomacy collapsed, were those of a train-passenger when his express thunders through the station at which he intended to alight. All of course except the Austrians. They were still waiting on the platform when, at their signal, the others had left for the battlefield.

(iii) *Great Britain on the Brink*

Eleven p.m. on 4 August 1914 was a moment of destiny for Great Britain. She had not been a military Power on a continental scale since the days of Marlborough. Her security had rested on the navy. The army had been an auxiliary, an expeditionary force. On that August night all was changed. How did it happen? What were the precise steps which led Great Britain into a major European war?

At the end of July she was still a free agent; her only binding commitment to action the old alliance with Portugal which had little practical importance. The Triple Entente with France and Russia was a partnership for diplomacy, not for war. It did not involve any pledge to action, and it had not prevented friendship with Germany.

The Conservatives, enjoying the freedom of opposition, often urged that the Triple Entente should be turned into a defensive alliance against Germany. Office might have made them less precise. The Liberal government at any rate refused to be tied. Some members of the Cabinet have been described as 'pacifists'. Perhaps one was: John Burns. The majority belonged rather to the same school as American isolationists. They did not believe that England could be endangered by events on the Continent. They had boundless faith in the British navy, so much so, indeed, that they often opposed increases in the naval estimates. And they thought that the best service which Great Britain could perform in Europe was to mediate between the contending Powers.

Asquith, the prime minister, and Grey, foreign secretary,

were less detached. They feared that Germany might have to
be resisted at some time in the future. They wanted to put
that time off, not to bring it on. They were procrastinators
by temperament and from conviction.

Asquith had kept a discordant cabinet together during six
troubled years. It had survived united and unharmed, despite
repeated stories of internal conflict and threats of resignation.
Asquith's method never varied. He sat placidly in cabinet
writing chatty letters to a lady friend until its members
argued themselves to a standstill. Then he would say inno-
cently: 'I think we are all agreed.'

Grey was attacked later by some colleagues, as he was
praised by opponents, for leading the country imperceptibly
into war. Radicals and Conservatives alike were mistaken.
Grey did not believe in leading the country anywhere. He
relied on events to shape his policy. He wrote of the August
crisis: 'There was little for me to do. Circumstances and
events were compelling decision.'

Of course Asquith and Grey could have produced a resolute foreign policy by breaking with their colleagues and
making a Coalition with the Conservatives. Such an idea
never crossed their minds. For one thing national unity
would have been lost. If the Liberal government went to
war, the Conservatives would support them. But if war were
started by a Coalition, most Liberals would go into fierce,
pacifist opposition.

Besides (a point Conservatives often forgot), Asquith and
Grey were Liberals themselves. They were deeply divided
from the Conservatives by the Irish crisis, and indeed in
later years kept independent Liberalism alive when their
Radical colleague, Lloyd George, was preaching permanent
Coalition. They had, too, a high opinion of their own capacity
to govern. Asquith had reached the point where he could not
imagine any other prime minister—a belief which was his
undoing in December 1916.

Grey often talked of resigning if his colleagues did not
support his policy. The point of this talk is often misunder-
stood. Grey did not mean that he would go into opposition.

He would withdraw from politics—as he professed eagerness to do—and would leave another Liberal to carry out a different policy. But, as Grey remained in office for ten years despite his longing for the trout-streams, it is not necessary to take his threats of resignation seriously.

During the diplomatic turmoil of July Grey preached moderation to all parties. He was clear that peace came before justice. Though he thought the Austrian demands on Serbia excessive, he also thought that Serbia should accept them rather than provoke a war. He wrote in his memoirs: 'It was better that Serbia should give way than that European peace should be broken'—exactly the attitude which Neville Chamberlain took towards Czechoslovakia twenty-four years later.

On 30 July Russia mobilized. Germany called on her to stop, then declared war on her. Grey's professional advisers urged him to back Russia—some from fear of a German, some from fear of a Russian, victory. Grey refused. He endorsed the almost unanimous cry of public opinion: keep out.

He went farther along the road to isolation. On 1 August he told the German ambassador: England will remain neutral if you promise not to attack France. This was potential dynamite. France was pledged to go to Russia's aid, though Grey did not know this—at any rate not in its precise terms. If the Germans had accepted Grey's offer, France, not Germany, would have appeared the aggressor. Yet Grey's plan would in fact have prevented the war. The French could even have promised not to aid Russia. For the Germans had no war plan against Russia, only a plan for knocking out France first. The rigours of a railway timetable dictated their refusal of Grey's offer.

Now it was clear that Germany would attack France. Grey still insisted that Great Britain was not pledged to intervene. On 2 August the leaders of the Opposition, Bonar Law and Lansdowne, wrote to Asquith, urging support for France and Russia. They promised 'the united support of the Opposition in all measures required by England's intervention in the war'. The Cabinet met at 11 a.m. Grey writes: 'The message from the Conservative leaders was first read and then laid aside; it could have no influence then on our discussion.' But the cabinet made a decision. It was proposed not by Grey, but by Morley, the leader of the non-intervention party: England would not allow the German fleet to enter the Channel and attack France.

This was a decision against war, not for it. It represented Morley's policy of 'diplomatic energy and armed neutrality'. Keeping the Germans out of the Channel rested on what Morley called 'the doorstep argument'. If there were no naval engagement on Great Britain's doorstep it was less likely that she would be drawn in.

All the cabinet except John Burns accepted Morley's proposal. Both French and Germans appreciated that the decision favoured Germany. Cambon, the French ambassador, was in despair; Tirpitz correspondingly delighted. He announced at once that the German fleet would not enter the Channel so long as Britain remained neutral.

The British cabinet met again at 6.30 p.m. on Sunday, 2 August. This time they discussed the question of Belgium. There was, as yet, no immediate alarm. No rumour of invasion had reached England or anywhere else. There was one danger signal. On 31 July Grey had asked both France and Germany to respect Belgian neutrality. The French had agreed. The Germans had not replied.

The British had feared a deal between Germany and Belgium. But on 1 August the Belgians declared that they would defend their neutrality. The way was clear for British backing. The Liberals had Gladstone for their master in foreign policy as in much else. They followed the precedent which he had laid down in 1870. Then a request that both sides respect Belgian neutrality had kept Great Britain out of war. So why not now?

The Cabinet resolved, just as Gladstone had, that 'a substantial violation of Belgian neutrality would compel us to take action'. The words were carefully chosen both in 1870 and 1914. The passage of German troops through Luxembourg or even through a corner of Belgian territory would not provoke British action. The resolution was another victory for the neutralists.

Later writers miss the key to the story and therefore find this explanation incredible. Yet the key is there for all to see. No one anywhere foresaw the massive German invasion of Belgium. No one knew that this was the only German war plan. No one in England foresaw it except, perhaps, Kitchener, who was about to depart disregarded for Egypt. The French did not foresee it. They planned an offensive on the narrow Franco-German front, an offensive which made sense only if there was no German move on the flank. The German government did not foresee it. Though Bethmann had been told vaguely of it years before, he had not taken it in and made no diplomatic preparations.

The Belgians foresaw it least of all. On 1 August they told Grey that their relations with all neighbouring Powers were excellent. They garrisoned their frontier against France as well as against Germany, just as the Swiss did. The people of Belgium spent the Sunday of 2 August enjoying the sun and rejoicing that, as a small neutral country, they would escape the clash of the Great Powers.

At 6.30 p.m. Below-Saleske, German representative in Brussels, telephoned for an immediate interview with Davignon, the foreign minister. He arrived at 7 p.m., pale and shaking. Davignon thought he was going to faint and asked: 'Are you not well?' Below replied: 'I climbed the stairs too quickly.' Then he read out an ultimatum that Germany must march through Belgium and demanding a reply within twelve hours. The paper dropped from his trembling hands to the floor. Davignon exclaimed: 'No. No, surely it is not possible.'

The Belgian Government met at nine and sat until 2.30 the following morning. They resolved to refuse the German demand and to defend their neutrality. But they still imagined that the Germans might retract. A resolute Belgian defence, still based on neutrality, would surely make the Germans think again. The Belgians did not therefore appeal to other Powers for support. On the contrary the Belgian troops were

ordered to fire on any French soldiers crossing the frontier.
The only appeal was from King Albert to George V for
'diplomatic intervention'.

On the following morning, August Bank Holiday, the
British cabinet met at 11 a.m. Grey produced the draft of his
speech to be made in the House that afternoon. It dealt
mainly with the proposal to keep the German fleet out of the
Channel. Just as the cabinet met a telegram arrived from
the British Minister at Brussels, giving news of the German
ultimatum. Morley resigned—in despair, not in protest. The
other non-interventionists were indignant at the German
demand. But they, too, went on dreaming that the Germans
would draw back if warned resolutely enough. With general
approval Grey tacked a passage about Belgium to his existing
draft.

The cabinet ended at 2 p.m. At 3 p.m. Grey spoke in the
House. His earlier part on France was a defence of his past
actions, feeble and apologetic. He still asked others to decide
policy for him: 'Let every man look into his own heart, and
his own feelings, and construe the extent of his obligation
for himself.' If this had been all, Grey would have had a
rough time. But the news about Belgium carried all before it.
The Radicals in the House, like those in the cabinet, swung
round.

Leaving the House, Churchill asked Grey: 'What happens
now?' Grey replied: 'Now we shall send them an ultimatum
to stop the invasion of Belgium within twenty-four hours.'
This sounds the sort of conversation that was made up afterwards. At any rate, nothing of the kind happened. The
cabinet met during the evening. It decided to ask the Germans for an assurance that their ultimatum would be withdrawn. There was no threat of war, no time limit. After the
cabinet Grey had dinner and went home to bed. The polite
request to Germany was sent off only at 9.30 a.m. on 4
August. It had still not crossed Grey's mind that there was
any urgency. After all, in the Crimean war—England's last
European war—there was a delay of two months between the
ultimatum and the declaration of war.

This time Grey's inquiry was out of date before it was sent. The first German troops crossed the Belgian frontier at 8 a.m. on 4 August. Agency reports of this reached London about midday. There was still no Belgian appeal for assistance. This reached London only at 12.50 a.m. on 5 August, almost two hours after Great Britain declared war. In fact we do not know why Grey decided to send an ultimatum. He did not consult the cabinet. Perhaps he consulted Asquith.

The ultimatum went off at 2 p.m. The Germans were again asked to respect the neutrality of Belgium. A satisfactory reply must 'be received here by twelve o'clock midnight'. The actual invasion of Belgian was not mentioned. The request was, of course, refused. At 7 p.m. Goschen, the British ambassador, saw Bethmann, who used a phrase that became famous. England, he said, was going to war 'just for a scrap of paper'. Did he use these very words? Did he speak in English or German? We shall never know; for when anyone thought of inquiring both men were dead. But we know that the phrase was already running in Goschen's mind. A fortnight earlier there had been private theatricals at his house; the play a piece by Sardou, its title in English: *A Scrap of Paper*.

Goschen obeyed instructions and asked for his passports. But no message from him reached London. The British Government would have been in an awkward hole if Bethmann had agreed to their demand, and the answer had been received only after they had declared war. We know that this was impossible. They did not. And leading Ministers sat in the cabinet room till the last moment, half-expecting a reply.

At some time in the evening a news agency announced that Germany had declared war on Great Britain. On the basis of this report, the German Ambassador was sent his passports at 10.15. The news then turned out to be false. A clerk from the foreign office (now Sir Harold Nicolson) hurried round to the German embassy; retrieved the British note; and substituted a new declaration of war, merely asserting that the German government had not replied. It was then 11.5 p.m.

The British declaration of war took effect at 11 p.m. Why? Eleven o'clock in London was midnight in Berlin. But the ultimatum asked for an answer *'Here* [i.e., in London] by twelve o'clock midnight.' What deprived the Germans of their last hour? Did someone fear that they might reply after all? Probably not. Just a blunder due to haste and muddle.

There was a final twist to the story. Great Britain had gone to war to defend the neutrality of Belgium. How to do it? This question had not been discussed by the cabinet nor by anyone else. Even now Asquith left it until 4 p.m. on 5 August. Then, in his capacity as acting secretary of state for war, he summoned a war council, which he rightly describes as 'a rather motley gathering'. The civilians were Grey, Haldane, Churchill; the soldiers, every distinguished general Asquith could lay hands on.

Lord Roberts, the senior of them, proposed to send the Expeditionary Force to Antwerp. Churchill answered that the navy could not guarantee a safe passage east of the Straits of Dover. No one remarked that it was impossible to go up the Scheldte without violating Dutch neutrality.

Sir John French, who was to command the B.E.F., suggested that the army might cross the Channel and then decide where to go—perhaps to Antwerp, perhaps to Amiens. Evidently he thought that it would be free to ramble round northern France, as he had rambled over the veldt in the Boer war. Haig thought that the expeditionary force should stop at home and train the mass armies of the future. It is easy to guess that he already saw himself as French's successor.

Sir Henry Wilson, director of military operations, grew more and more impatient. The war council seemed to him 'an historic meeting of men mostly entirely ignorant of their subject'. He now struck in. There was, he insisted, no choice. Once more railway timetables dictated policy. The B.E.F. could not help the Belgians. It could only go to Maubeuge on the left wing of the French army. The marshalling-yards were prepared, trucks ready, lines cleared. It was Maubeuge or nothing.

The discussion ended. The next day, 6 August, the cabinet agreed to the sending of the B.E.F., but decided that it should go to Amiens. No one took any notice. The timetable said Maubeuge. And to Maubeuge it went.

In this strange way the Conservative Opposition won. The B.E.F. did nothing to help Belgium, though this was why the Liberal cabinet had gone to war. It went to aid the French, which the Radical majority in the cabinet had been resolved not to do. Of course neither the Conservative leaders nor Sir Henry Wilson foresaw that the B.E.F., instead of acting as a reserve on the remote left of a great battle, would find itself plumb in the track of the whole German army. . . .

VIII

THE WAR AIMS OF THE ALLIES
IN THE FIRST WORLD WAR

NONE of the Great Powers entered the war of 1914 with
defined war aims. Each took up arms for an ostensibly
defensive reason, and the programme of each was limited at
first to victory in the field. All anticipated short decisive
battles and expected the war to be over by Christmas. These
expectations were not fulfilled, and the belligerents found
themselves, unwillingly enough, with time on their hands to
define what they were fighting for as well as what they were
fighting against. The Germans had the easier task. They had
won the first campaigns, though not the war itself, and their
war programme boiled down to keeping all or part of what
they had gained—control over Belgium and north-eastern
France, domination of the Balkans or, in more general terms,
a consolidated *Mitteleuropa*. The Germans made only tactical
variations in these aims until October 1918. The Entente
Powers found it harder to be precise. In one way, they were
less pressed for terms. While the Germans wanted to end a
war which they had already won, the Allies would not be
called on for their terms until they had reversed the effect of
the first German victories. Until the end the practical war
aim of the French was to expel the Germans from 'the national
territory'; of the British to liberate Belgium; of the Russians
to survive as a great military Power.

The Allies could not maintain this negative position. A
purely defensive war lacked inspiration. The peoples demanded the prospect of a better world; and the need for this was
reinforced when the Allies, Great Britain in particular,

appealed to public opinion in the United States. Further, the Allies needed to define their war aims towards each other. In 1815 Gentz cynically described the task of the congress of Vienna as 'dividing among the victors the spoils of the vanquished'; and, though this was an exaggeration in regard to the settlement of Vienna, or even in regard to that of 1919, relations among victors certainly change fundamentally when the vanquished fall out of the balance. The Russians were well aware that Great Britain and France had sought their friendship mainly, if not solely, from fear of Germany; the French appreciated that their disputes with Great Britain in the Near East were likely to be renewed once German power disappeared. Moreover, the French and the Russians—both heavily engaged against Germany—feared that Great Britain might steal a march on them elsewhere in the world; and though the British could not help doing this, they wished to give their allies an assurance against it all the same.

War aims were, in fact, weapons of war. The public programmes were designed to maintain morale and to win American approval; the secret treaties to give the Allies confidence in each other. Like most treaties, they were a promise that their relations would remain the same when the circumstances which caused these relations altered. Later on, when the secret treaties became known and when the peace settlement aroused perhaps unreasonable disappointment, it was widely held that the secret treaties expressed the real war aims of the Allied rulers and that the public programmes were a fraud on the Allied peoples, on the Americans, and even on the Germans. This was not so. The secret treaties did not contain Allied war aims in the strict sense. They attempted rather to secure the relations of the Allies between themselves; they defined solutions for the problems which would follow the defeat of Germany, not the objects for which Germany should be defeated. It is not surprising, in the circumstances, that the secret treaties were made. What is surprising is that these treaties clashed so little with the public statements. And most surprising of all that the Allies managed to reach a general, even an idealistic, programme when their only practical aim remained, to the end, the defeat of Germany.

The British were the first to begin the process of definition. In Russia the imperial government did not trouble much about public opinion and used only the old slogans of Holy Russia and a Life for the Tsar. In France parliamentary government was suspended until the end of 1914, and everything subordinated to national defence. Parliamentary life went on in England, and with it a free press. There was also the peculiar circumstance that a Liberal government was in power; and until the very last minute the principal newspapers supporting the government had been the most opposed to war. Now these same newspapers had to show why they were the most strenuous in supporting the war. It is a great mistake to suppose that the two wings of the Liberal party welcomed estrangement from each other. Perhaps Lloyd George had sometimes thought of splitting the party and putting himself at the head of a Radical-Labour coalition, but he had not done it. And on the other side, if Asquith or Grey had really felt himself nearer to the Conservatives than to the Radicals, he would have gone over to the Conservatives; neither did so. All Liberals rejoiced that the war had reunited them; and the basis of this reunion had to be an idealistic programme. The great Liberal editors, such as Scott of the *Manchester Guardian* and A. G. Gardiner of the *Daily News*, recognized indeed that war was a defeat for Liberalism and a victory for the evil forces which they personified in Lord Northcliffe; but they believed that this defeat could be transformed into a victory if war was made to serve some nobler cause.

Scott had a hard core of realism. He concentrated on winning the war once he had failed to avert it—hence his support two years later for the Lloyd George-Bonar Law coalition even against Asquith and the bulk of the Liberal party. When the *Manchester Guardian* looked towards the future early in 1915, Scott called on the moderate L. T. Hobhouse, and that wise man spoke out against any early reconciliation with Germany. 'The peacemakers will err

seriously if they set to work after the war as though the
revelation of the mind of German statesmanship were to
count for nothing.' Hobhouse wanted the Triple Entente to
become a permanent federation, holding all the power in
Europe. He was not afraid to hold out the example of the
Holy Alliance and warned that this failed only when its
idealism became too dogmatically international. The Supreme
Council of the Allies, he thought later, should control Europe.
In time the neutrals could be added with a subordinate voice,
and last of all the defeated Powers.

Gardiner was not so cautious. On 8 August he repudiated
any quarrel with the German people and announced 'we are
fighting for the emancipation of Germany'. He had already
hit on a simple explanation of the conflict: 'this is not a
war of peoples but of despots and diplomatists'. H. G. Wells
added his voice. 'The defeat of Germany will open the door
to disarmament and peace throughout the earth.' On 7
August he called the war the *Sword of Peace*. On 14 August
he did even better. He invented the phrase which was to
echo round the world, at first as an inspiration, later in bitter
mockery. He discovered *The War to End War*. There
would be 'a Peace League that will control the globe'. A
little later Eden Phillpotts held out the same prospect to the
Germans in more high-flown terms:

> And our revenge shall be to bid you hear
> Ineffable music from the olden time.

Yet there was no cleavage between the idealists and
the practical statesmen except in their mode of expression.
The outlook of Lowes Dickinson, who invented the phrase 'the
League of Nations' and who (as his so-called historical works
show) did not blame one nation more than another for the
war, shaded imperceptibly into that of Gilbert Murray or
H. G. Wells, who were convinced that the war had been
caused by German militarism; and their outlook in turn
shaded into that of Grey and Asquith. No British statesman
would be content with the liberation or restoration of Belgium, though this had given the occasion for the war. Grey,

for instance, said in November 1914 that there could be no peace that would permit 'continuance or recurrence of an armed brute power in central Europe'; the future peace must provide for 'an end of militarism for ever and for reparation to ruined Belgium'.

Certain practical conditions were already foreshadowed. Since final victory was assumed, the disappearance of the German fleet was assumed also, and it seemed unnecessary to stipulate this in the peace terms. The acquisition of the German colonies was assumed in the same casual way. But what should happen on the continent of Europe? Gladstone provided the ultimate inspiration for Liberal foreign policy. He had not only believed in the national principle; he had sympathized with Russian aims and had protested against the German annexation of Alsace and Lorraine. All the Liberal writers insisted that Alsace and Lorraine should return to France, though the most Radical (such as Brailsford) wanted this to be preceded by a plebiscite. Most of them supported 'a Greater Servia' and Rumanian claims to Transylvania, though Rumania was neutral. The only other concrete grievance they discovered was that of the 'Bulgarians' under Serbia in Macedonia—certainly even-handed justice against an ally. H. G. Wells held that 'an unchallenged Russia will be a wholesome check and no great danger for the new Greater Servia and the new Greater Roumania'. Only Brailsford dissented: 'Within a year from the breaking of Germany's power . . ., our Imperialists will be calling out for a strong Germany to balance a threatening Russia.' The statesmen agreed with the writers. Asquith regarded the ethnographical principle as 'the only one which was serious and lasting'—a phrase which Tsar Nicholas II underlined with satisfaction. Grey approved the French claim to Alsace and Lorraine, though there was, as yet, no British commitment to France on this point. He, too, sought concessions to Bulgaria and to Rumania—perhaps more to win them as allies than to satisfy abstract justice.

The French began to define their war aims only towards the end of the year when the first shock of battle was over.

D

They too wanted a settled peace for the future, but in their case it was precise security against Germany, not a general system of world order. Delcassé spoke of 'the destruction of the German Reich and the weakening of Prussia'; Viviani described the war as 'defence against the German desire to control Europe'. On 22 December Deschanel, president of the Chamber, first formally laid claim to Alsace and Lorraine. He brought in also the liberation of Belgium, but the emphasis was not so strong as it was in British policy. The British regarded Belgium as a special case which came before all else. The French lumped together Belgium and north-eastern France (in which they included Alsace and Lorraine), and they unconsciously extended to their own territory the 'massive reparation' which the British projected for Belgium alone. Farther east the French were a good deal less enthusiastic than the British about 'the national principle'. They dreamt of some miracle by which the defeat of Germany would not involve the defeat of Austria-Hungary also; they cared less for Serbia than for Poland—a subject remote from British speculation; and they fondly supposed that Russia's ambitions would be met by 'the freedom of the Straits'.

The Russians had certainly not formulated a clear picture of their aims even at the Straits when they entered the war. But, with their incurable taste for future precision to offset their present confusions, they were the first to sketch a programme of territorial changes. Early in September Sazonov, the foreign minister, defined his guiding principles as 'destruction of German power and the principle of nationality'. Russia would take eastern Galicia and advance to the line of the Niemen. Poland, conveniently under Russian suzerainty, would take eastern Posen, Silesia and west Galicia. France, of course, would recover Alsace and Lorraine. Belgium would acquire some German territory; Sleswig and Holstein would return to Denmark; and the kingdom of Hanover would be restored—as much to please the British royal house as to weaken Prussia. The Habsburg monarchy would be dismembered into three Succession States—

Austria, Bohemia, Hungary. Rumania would receive 'part of Transylvania', but not Bessarabia on any account ('not an inch of Russian land' was Nicholas II's phrase). Serbia would receive Bosnia and Hercegovina, Dalmatia and northern Albania; Greece, southern Albania; and Bulgaria part of Macedonia. In short, the full national programme of small independent states—except for Poland—but no word of the Straits. Later in the autumn the Russian experts tried to formulate a solution for the Straits question, but arrived only at the conclusion that all plans were equally bad. Even 'the active solution' of a Russian occupation of Constantinople would so absorb Russia's resources as to leave her without strength elsewhere. Better to be content with the vague aims of 'destroying German and Austrian attempts to challenge Russia's prestige as a Great Power' and 'freeing Europe from militarism'.

These speculations were far removed from a policy. There was no serious exchange of ideas between the Entente Powers on war aims during the first winter of the war. Since they also failed to exchange ideas even on the conduct of the war, this is not surprising. The only tie between them was the treaty signed on 5 September 1914, by which the three Powers promised not to make a separate peace nor to pose peace terms to the enemy without previous agreement. This was, in fact, the only real commitment ever made by the Entente Powers. It was not necessary to act on it until some prospect of peace negotiations appeared, and by then Russia was out of the war. But Russia was pushed into making practical demands early in 1915, though more against her allies than against the enemy. The British project for forcing the Dardanelles—though originally provoked by the Russian generals—alarmed the diplomats; they feared that Constantinople might fall from the feeble hands of the Turks into those of the western Powers. On 4 March, without preliminary warning, Sazonov informed the French and British ambassadors in writing that 'any solution would be unsatisfactory and precarious' which did not give Constantinople and the shores of the Bosphorus to Russia.

'The Imperial government hopes that these considerations will be treated sympathetically by the allied Powers.'

The Russians expected resistance from the British. They were mistaken. The British had long written off their old interest in the Straits. They were now impatient to launch the Dardanelles campaign and, lacking trained soldiers themselves, were anxious to keep Russia active on the eastern Front. A Russian attempt to reach Constantinople first (in fact, regarded by the Russian General Staff as impracticable) would have much disturbed British policy. On 12 March Grey, with the approval of the Opposition leaders, Lansdowne, Bonar Law and Balfour, declared British approval of Russia's claims 'subject to the war being carried on and brought to a successful conclusion and to the desiderata of Great Britain and France in the Ottoman empire and elsewhere being realized'. He followed this up the same day with some immediate conditions: Constantinople should become a free port; the Mohammedan Holy Places and Arabia should remain under independent Mohammedan dominion; and the neutral zone of Persia, as defined in the agreement of 1907, should become a British sphere. On 20 March Sazonov agreed to these conditions, with some slight adjustments in Persia and a free hand for Russia in her own zone.

The French turned out much more difficult. Delcassé persistently deluded himself that the Russians would be satisfied with internationalization of the Straits. Faced with Sazonov's demand, he offered only 'a friendly attitude' and a reminder that the Straits, along with all other questions, must be settled by common discussion according to the agreement of 5 September 1914. When this met with a cool reception, he fell back on the excuse that England would never agree to the Russian claims. Disappointed here also, he tried delay. On 5 April 'he struck his forehead and said that he had forgotten to send instructions to St. Petersburg'. There was no averting the inevitable. On 10 April the French Government also declared their agreement to Russia's claims on similar conditions to those that the British had made on 12 March. But, in the gloom of giving way, the French failed to define these conditions. The Russians had been generous during the period of delay. Nicholas II had said: 'take the left back of the Rhine; take Mainz; go further if you like'. He had agreed to support French claims to Syria, Cilicia and Palestine—with some reserve over the Holy Places. Delcassé failed to take up these offers. The French were so angry at having to give way over Constantinople and the Straits that they did it finally without claiming a reward. If they had struck a bargain in April 1915 they would have had Russian backing when they came to negotiate over the Near East with Great Britain. As it was, the Russians were free to join with the British in forcing further compromises on the French.

The agreement over Constantinople and the Straits, though later the most maligned of the secret treaties, was not strictly a war aim at all. It did not lay down terms which the Entente would impose on the enemy; it only defined what they would settle between themselves if they won the war. The Treaty of London with Italy which followed shortly after had a different character. It laid down what Italy 'will receive', and this certainly implied an obligation on the Entente Powers to continue fighting until Italy's aims were achieved. Russia was already at war; she had only to be persuaded to remain there. Italy was a neutral; she had to be brought in, and the French, at any rate, considered that she would be a decisive gain. The Italians claimed Tyrol, Trieste with Istria, and Dalmatia. The British and French made no objection. These were all traditional objects of Italian nationalism; and support for them no more implied approval for the dismemberment of Austria-Hungary than had support for the unification of Italy fifty or sixty years before. Sazonov, fearing a new rival at the Straits, did not want Italy in the war. He was overruled by his western allies and by his own general staff. He held firm only over southern Dalmatia which he insisted should go to Serbia. This was a fine display of Slav solidarity; more immediately, southern Dalmatia was the price with which Sazonov hoped to persuade Serbia into surrendering Macedonia to Bulgaria.

The Allies were certainly tied to Italy's war aims by the Treaty of London. It was a more important consideration that Italy was tied to them also. Once having staked her claims she could not recede from them. She was the most opposed of the Entente Powers to the dismemberment of Austria-Hungary; yet she had to pursue her claims even at the price of this dismemberment, and became finally the most intransigent Entente Power so far as Austria-Hungary was concerned.

The Russians tried to stave off Italian intervention in the Ottoman empire before the Treaty of London was signed. They proposed to stipulate that Italy should endorse the agreement of the Triple Entente over the Straits without seeing it. This was too much. Indeed the Treaty of London promised 'an equitable share' of Asia Minor to Italy; but Great Britain and France formally reaffirmed to Russia their pledge over the Straits when Italy entered the war. The pledge was thus directed now against Italy as well as against themselves. The French had a more pressing anxiety. They wished to define the plans concerning the Ottoman empire which they had made Russia endorse. But this demanded negotiations with the British, and they had plans of their own in the Near East. They had already promised the Sherif of Mecca that Arabia should be an independent State in order to bring him into war; and they interpreted 'Arabia' generously, so long as it did not extend to the valley of the Euphrates. Grey evaded negotiation with the French at the time of the Straits agreement. They renewed their insistence in the autumn, when Georges Picot came to London to negotiate with Sir Mark Sykes. The French assumed that the British would be content with Mesopotamia, and they intended to claim for themselves Syria, Cilicia and Palestine.

This did not meet with British approval. They demanded Haifa for themselves, as outlet for a railway from Bagdad; Beirut for the 'independent' Arab State; and, most serious of all, Palestine as an international State. In the agreement with Russia Grey had stipulated only for the independence of the Mohammedan Holy Places; it now turned out that he had felt as strongly about the Christian Holy Places and, when Picot protested, Sykes answered that Russia would never agree to their passing under French control. This was a curious revival of the great issue in the Crimean war, but with Russia and Great Britain this time in alliance against France. The French would be left with a thin strip of Mediterranean coastline, deprived of its best ports. Sykes finally gave up Beirut, and, as Picot was still dissatisfied, he added a platonic approval to any extension of claims in Armenia that the French cared to make. This would put a wedge of French influence between the British sphere in Mesopotamia and the Russian sphere in northern Persia, and Kitchener laid down the proposition that it was undesirable for the British 'to be in immediate contact with a great military monarchy'. In this way the French, without knowing it, received title (temporary as it turned out) to the oilfields of Mosul.

The Sykes-Picot Agreement, signed on 3 January 1916, postulated the approval of Russia. Sazonov offered to sign it blindfold on 19 February. The western Powers did not take him at his word, principally because each wished to play Russia off against the other. Sykes and Picot came to Petrograd armed with invitations for Russian backing. Sykes gave Sazonov a map marked with objections that he might usefully make; Picot persuaded Sazonov to promise to oppose the British plans for Palestine—a promise which he did not fulfil. For, when the Russians looked at the agreements, they were horrified to see the French claims in Armenia, which extended even to the frontier of the Russian zone in Persia. Henceforth Sazonov was busy opposing the French claims and had no time to worry about Palestine. Sykes joined Sazonov, and the two forced concession on Picot. The French line was withdrawn in Armenia; in exchange it extended somewhat farther north in Cilicia, into purely Turkish territory. More striking still, Sykes and Picot, in their anxiety for Russia's approval, acquiesced in her claiming the whole of Armenia—rather to the annoyance of the Russian general staff, who regarded it as too big a morsel and who were, in any case, incapable of conquering it. In this way Russia was paid twice over for agreeing to the Anglo-French partition of the Near East: beforehand with Constantinople and the Straits, afterwards with Armenia. Yet at bottom the Russians did not want either price; they wanted 'a Turkey as large and independent as possible' as a buffer between themselves and any western Powers.

The three allies reached general agreement in April 1916 on these questions; points of drafting, such as the future of the Capitulations and the open door for trade, dragged on until September, and even then some details remained unsettled. This agreement over Asiatic Turkey was also not strictly a war aim. It too merely laid down what each would allow the others to do when the Ottoman empire collapsed. There was no promise of mutual support, though, of course, an implied condition that one ally could not claim his full share if the others were disappointed. Though the agreements were secret, the two western Powers would have liked to make them public—the French to show their own people that they were not being cheated in the Near East, and both governments to encourage Russia to remain in the war. Asquith hinted at the agreements when a Russian parliamentary delegation visited England in May; and the agreement over the Straits was described in the Duma in December—without any effect on Russian war-weariness. All this talk alarmed the Italians. They saw themselves being left out of the partition of the Near East and claimed the fulfilment of the promise made to them in the Treaty of London. The Allies insisted that Italy must first declare war on Germany, which she did in August 1916. Now it was the turn of the original Allies to hesitate. They feared rightly an Italian explosion when it was revealed that the Ottoman empire was already partitioned. Grey finally persuaded his two partners that the agreements should be regarded as binding only when Italy declared herself satisfied. No doubt he would not have lamented if the condition were never fulfilled.

The Italians were told of the Asiatic agreements on 5 October. They were indignant and answered by demanding for themselves a zone of Asia Minor which, on the one side, would take Adana and Mersina from the French zone and, on the other, would, at Smyrna, approach dangerously near the Russian territory at the Straits. The British made no objection. The French and Russians, however, were united in opposition, and a conference at London met with complete deadlock early in 1917. Meanwhile the discussion of genuine war aims had begun in earnest. This sprang from the increasing desire of the western Powers to draw in the United States. Quite apart from the practical need for American assistance, the Allies—Great Britain in particular —looked to America for help in providing some stabler basis of peace than mere victory. The Allies still thought that they could win the war; but then the United States should, in Grey's words, 'come into some general guaranty for world-wide peace'. Grey returned to this idea again and again. He wrote on 22 September 1915: 'would the President propose a League of Nations binding themselves to side against any Power which broke a treaty?'

This was not far from Wilson's own outlook. Though determined to preserve American neutrality in the present war, he hoped also to act as the guarantor of a future peace, provided this were enlightened enough. His ideas for such a peace corresponded closely with those of the English Liberals, for he too was a Gladstonian. He too regarded the German annexation of Alsace and Lorraine as a crime. He declared: 'Russia's ambitions are legitimate', and said: 'I cannot help sympathizing with Russia's aims to secure natural outlets for its trade with the world.' He did not share the fears of his adviser House about Russia and wrote in December 1914: 'Austria-Hungary will go to pieces altogether—ought to go to pieces for the welfare of Europe.' He was constantly hinting that the Allies should announce enlightened war aims so that he could then prepare to guarantee them. Early in 1916 the British tried to oblige him. Asquith, Grey, Lloyd George, and Balfour met House at Lord Reading's and sketched terms which House thought the president would approve: 'the restoration of Belgium,

D*

the transfer of Alsace and Lorraine to France, and the acquisition by Russia of an outlet to the sea'. There was, however,
an equivocation. Wilson only meant to guarantee these
terms after the Allies had won the war—and then only if
they behaved generously in other ways. The British ministers
hoped to lure Wilson into imposing these terms on Germany,
and House encouraged their delusion.

In August 1916 Grey told the American ambassador that
there could be no discussion of peace terms until France
agreed, and added a new condition: 'an impartial enquiry
who began the war and who is responsible for it?' This
academic point was not pursued. Meanwhile the British
went on speculating what they should propose either to the
French or for themselves. Robertson, chief of the general
staff, produced a memorandum on 31 August, saying that
Alsace and Lorraine must 'presumably' go to France. But
Austria-Hungary should be kept in being: 'this limits the
power of Russia and the Slav states, and prevents the Mediterranean becoming a French and Italian lake'. In general, 'it
is in the interests of the British empire to leave Germany
reasonably strong on land, but to weaken her at sea'—a
curious outlook for one who held that all British effort should
be concentrated on the western Front. Balfour followed on
4 October with a very different policy. He wanted to reduce
the Central Powers and to apply everywhere 'the principle of
nationality'—in Alsace and Lorraine, and for the benefit of
Italy, Serbia and Rumania. 'I should greatly like to see it
applied in Bohemia also.' But he would *not* like to see the
old kingdom of Poland restored. 'If Germany is relieved of
all fear of pressure from Russia, France and Britain might be
the sufferers and Russia might be diverted to the Far East.'
He waved aside all fear of Russia: 'The more Russia is made
a European rather than an Asiatic power the better for
everybody. . . . Whatever trouble Russia may give us in
Mesopotamia, Persia and Afghanistan, I do not think she will
attempt the domination of Europe, still less succeed in
securing it.'

The two continental allies were also revolving these

problems. The Russians had by now little interest in general principles. Their greatest anxiety during the course of 1916 was to ward off any suggestion of Polish independence by their western allies. Sazonov said to Paléologue, the French ambassador, in March: 'Beware of Poland. It is dangerous ground for an ambassador of France.' Sazonov hit on the idea of buying off French interest in Poland by the offer of a free hand for France on the western frontier of Germany— an idea which he did little to develop before his fall from power in July. The French became alarmed that Russia was moving towards a separate peace, and they, in turn, contemplated offering Russia a free hand on Germany's eastern frontier. Briand, the French prime minister, soon thought better of this. He was becoming the protagonist of national independence—the first French statesman to make the liberation of Serbia a war aim (3 November 1915), and the first Allied statesman to receive Beneš, representative of the future Czechoslovakia (February 1916). It ill became him to renounce French interest in Poland; or, if he did so, it must be cloaked by some striking French gain—in other words, the left bank of the Rhine. Both Grey and Briand were thus moving towards a formulation of war aims—Grey principally to interest the Americans, Briand more to console the Russians.

In September 1916 Briand offered to undertake the task. He had not completed it when the Entente was caught unawares by President Wilson's note of 18 December, which invited both sides to state their peace terms. The British at first wanted to reject the suggestion. Lloyd George called it 'a sort of insult' to put both sides on the same level. Briand, however, pulled out his unfinished draft, adding to it a protest 'against the assimilation established in the American note between the two groups of belligerents'. Briand's note declared that it was impossible to discuss peace terms until there was 'a satisfactory settlement of the present conflict', and he confined himself to the general principles of 'reparation, restitution and guarantees'. The British now took up the running. At the inter-allied conference in London on

27–28 December they objected that the Allies would be suspected of shady designs if they did not state some concrete aims. Ribot, who represented France, was a more practical man than Briand and agreed with them. A new paragraph of concrete aims was therefore tacked on, though Briand's assertion of the impossibility of defining such aims still remained to contradict it. This paragraph had then to be settled with the Russians and the Italians. Balfour had proposed to refer to 'a free autonomous Poland'. The Russians objected, and the issue was dodged. The Italians objected to including 'the South Slavs' in the list of nationalities to be liberated. The more harmless word 'Slav' was substituted; but to make the list look more practical the 'Czecho-Slovaks' were added, though without any realization that this implied the destruction of the Habsburg monarchy.

This note was handed to the Americans on 10 January 1917. It demanded 'the restoration of Belgium, of Serbia and of Montenegro and the indemnities which are due them; the evacuation of the invaded territories . . .; the reorganization of Europe, guaranteed by a stable régime and founded as much upon respect of nationalities . . . as upon territorial conventions and international agreements'. Then came the practical aims: 'the restitution of provinces or territories wrested in the past from the Allies by force . . ., the liberation of Italians, of Slavs, of Roumanians and of Czecho-Slovaks from foreign domination; the enfranchisement of populations subject to the bloody tyranny of the Turks; the expulsion from Europe of the Ottoman Empire'. Finally, 'the intentions of His Majesty the Emperor of Russia regarding Poland have been clearly indicated in the proclamation which he has just addressed to his armies'. This list had some curiosities. Alsace and Lorraine were mentioned only by implication—though what other provinces or territories had been wrested from the Allies by force? Belgium was put on a level with Serbia and Montenegro despite her protests. The partition of the Ottoman empire appeared in an idealistic Gladstonian dress. And the future of Poland remained at Russia's discretion.

Neither the British nor the French Government was happy about this note. Both wished to underline some of its implications. On 13 January Balfour, who had recently become foreign secretary, followed it up by a supplementary note to Washington, justifying at length 'the expulsion of the Turks from Europe' and the dismemberment of the Ottoman empire. He also laid down three conditions for a durable peace (apart from 'the success of the Allied cause' as a preliminary): 'existing causes of international unrest should be, as far as possible, removed or weakened'; 'the aggressive aims and the unscrupulous methods of the Central Powers should fall into disrepute among their own people'; 'behind international law and all treaty arrangements . . . some form of international sanction should be devised which would give pause to the hardiest aggressor'. The Americans were being offered an effective League of Nations such as Wilson had often proposed, and were given to understand that the partition of the Ottoman empire was Great Britain's only concrete war aim. Lloyd George supplied a further gloss in February. Asked by Lansing, the American secretary of state, for assurances against the 'virtual dismemberment of Austria-Hungary', he answered that 'the peoples of the Entente Governments such as Slavs, Roumanians, Serbs and Italians, as well as Bosnia and Herzegovina, must by the principle of nationality be freed from Austrian control'; but Bohemia and Hungary would remain intact—not only a contradiction of his previous sentence, but a repudiation of the declaration made on 10 January in favour of the Czechoslovaks. Lloyd George added the curious remark that he wanted to see the United States at the peace conference in order to check the colonial demands of South Africa and Australia, and even of the British people.

Briand defined his aims in a letter to Paul Cambon at London on 12 January. Alsace and Lorraine should go to France not as a conquest but as a 'disannexation', and this should include the valley of the Saar. The German territory on the left bank of the Rhine should form a neutral buffer State. For the rest, Belgium should be restored; Denmark should receive Sleswig; Poland should become autonomous; Rumania and Serbia should make 'legitimate acquisitions'. Evidently Briand did not regard Italian ambitions as a French war aim, and he remained discreetly silent about Constantinople. He had also different views about the League of Nations. Where the British wanted a general system of security, Briand projected a league of victors. The Entente 'should be united more closely by treaties of alliance, in order to compose permanently an association of strength which would make itself respected'. This was much the policy which Hobhouse had advocated against the weight of Liberal opinion. Briand's statement was met in London with disapproving silence.

With Russia Briand did rather better—or so he thought. An inter-allied conference met at Petrograd in February 1917. Its main purpose was to coordinate Allied military plans and to keep Russia in the war. But the French had also policy in view. For one thing, they wanted Russia to join them in resisting Italian claims in Asia Minor: if the Russians would keep the Italians out of Mersina and Adana, the French would keep them out of Smyrna. For another thing, the French wanted Russian backing for their scheme to make a buffer state on the left bank of the Rhine. Doumergue, the French delegate, had as instructions only Briand's letter to Paul Cambon of 12 January. He got nothing from the Russians concerning Asia Minor except an exclamation of disapproval about Smyrna; but he did exceptionally well over the left bank of the Rhine. No sooner did he raise the subject than the tsar endorsed every French demand: Alsace and Lorraine and the Saar in full sovereignty; the left bank 'an autonomous and neutral state' occupied by French troops until the enemy states had completely fulfilled all conditions and guarantees laid down in the peace treaties. The Russian ministers were taken aback by their master's precipitancy; he had promised to support the French demands without claiming anything for Russia in return. However, they soon put matters right. They stated their claims in Paris, and Briand, out of touch with Doumergue and unwilling to wreck his

negotiations, agreed to them. He tried to postulate something about the future of Poland, was overruled, and on 12
March gave Russia 'full freedom to determine her western
frontiers'.

The Russian Revolution soon deprived this agreement of
any meaning. The revolution had more serious effects. The
new Russian leaders were soon talking of a peace with 'no
annexations and no indemnities', and this phrase forced
western statesmen into idealistic competition. On a more
practical level, Russia was obviously tumbling out of the war,
and this made Italy more important to the western Allies. As
a further complication, the new Austrian emperor, Charles,
made a secret offer of peace to the French in March. The
Austrians recognized that the Entente had certain claims
against Germany—Alsace-Lorraine and the restoration of
Belgium; some claims against Austria-Hungary in favour of
the Serbs, Rumanians and Italians; and, finally, the Straits
to Russia. Charles proposed to endorse the claims against
Germany on conditions that the Entente dropped those
against Austria-Hungary, and he would even support the
western Powers against Russia. Lloyd George and Ribot
were tempted by these proposals. They made some slight
reservation in regard to Serbia, but none in regard to Rumania
—despite the formal pledge to support her claims which
France had made the previous year when Rumania entered
the war. Neither had qualms about the Straits, the French
indeed much pleasure at thwarting Russia, and both statesmen welcomed the prospect of making a purely European
peace without either Russia or the United States—neither
of whom was informed of the negotiations.

Italy, however, had to be won over. For she was, after all,
the only Power actually fighting Austria-Hungary. On the
other hand, Lloyd George and Ribot were pledged not to
reveal to Italy that they were negotiating with Emperor
Charles. They therefore invited Sonnino, the Italian prime
minister, to meet them at St. Jean de Maurienne on 19 April,
ostensibly to resolve the deadlock in the negotiations over
Asia Minor. Sonnino refused to depart in the slightest from

the Italian claims which had been recognized in the Treaty of London; this made it pointless even to hint at the possibility of a separate peace with Austria. But the British were anxious to get Italian agreement over Asia Minor. They were caught by their ingenious argument of the previous autumn that the agreements should become effective only when Italy acquiesced; for now, with Russia almost out of the war, they needed Italian support against France. Earlier the British had worked with Russia in order to diminish France's share and especially to keep her out of Palestine. Now Russia was useless, and the British were indifferent to her claims. When Sonnino continued obstinate, Lloyd George withdrew from the room and returned with a British staff map on which Smyrna (hitherto a Russian interest) was allotted to Italy. Sonnino pulled out another copy of the same map, which the British had put forward at the London Conference of the previous January, and on which the gain to Italy was Konia, adjacent to the French sphere. He then agreed to take both, while Ribot and Lloyd George sat by in bewildered admiration.

No formal agreement was reached at St. Jean de Maurienne, though the letters exchanged later in August conventionally bear its name. The Italians continued to demand precision throughout the summer. When the French delayed, the British suggested a direct Anglo-Italian agreement, which would, of course, have been pointed against the French. This spurred the French to action, and letters defining the spheres of interest of the three countries were exchanged on 18 August. The French belatedly insisted on Russian approval —to wreck the agreements rather than to please their failing ally. The agreement therefore began with the words, 'under reserve of Russian assent'. No reply came from Russia before the Bolshevik Revolution of November put an end to allied relations. The agreements over the Ottoman empire remained in considerable confusion. The French and the British held that the so-called agreement of St. Jean de Maurienne had lapsed from lack of Russian approval, and they never acknowledged Italy's claim again. But was it the only agreement that lapsed when Russia fell out of the war? The original

Sykes-Picot agreement of January 1916 was a consequence of the Straits agreement made in March 1915 and postulated Russian approval also. This was obtained in May 1916 when the Sykes-Picot agreement was superseded by a three-sided exchange of letters. Did not Russia's renunciation of the Straits cast some doubt on the other agreements? In particular, could the Sykes-Picot agreement be resurrected as though later negotiations had never been?

These questions were to cause much trouble at the end of the war. Meanwhile the British put increasing emphasis on their promises of national independence to the Arabs— promises which they intended should operate against the French, but not against themselves. They also took new precautions in regard to Palestine, which was dangerously near the Suez Canal. The Holy Places had been effective in keeping France out of Palestine so long as Russia was both Orthodox and an active belligerent. When Russia became first a secular republic and then fell out of the war, the British needed some other instrument. They found it in Zionism. On 8 November, one day after the Bolshevik Revolution, Balfour announced that 'His Majesty's Government view with favour the establishment in Palestine of a national home for the Jewish people', and the British were soon talking of Palestine as a national State without reserve—which indeed it became when enough Jews were persuaded to settle there. Abraham and David succeeded where the saints of the Orthodox church had failed. Palestine became a British, not a French care.

The partition of the Ottoman empire was a side issue, however fascinating to the respective foreign offices. The great purpose of war aims became increasingly to satisfy public opinion in the Allied countries and in the United States. On 6 April the United States entered the war, though as an associate, not an ally. Balfour went over to Washington. While there, he discussed war aims with House and, more vaguely, with Wilson. On 28 April he showed House a map with the projected partition of Turkey in Asia and ran over the usual points—Alsace-Lorraine; restitution and reparation of all occupied territory; Bosnia and Hercegovina for Serbia; Macedonia for Bulgaria. House and Balfour differed over Poland. House wanted it as a strong barrier against Russia, and asked Balfour 'not to look upon Germany as a permanent enemy'. Balfour, however, 'was more impressed with the German menace than he was by the possible danger from Russia'. House also told Balfour that the proposals for Turkey in Asia were 'all bad'. Balfour was unrepentant, but did not scruple to jettison British commitments elsewhere. He 'regretted the Treaty of London', and agreed with House that Constantinople should be 'internationalized'. Evidently he regarded the secret treaties as a statement of aims by the ally concerned, with no obligation by Great Britain to support them, nor even perhaps not to oppose them.

On 30 April Balfour and President Wilson also surveyed the future, agreeing only on 'the internationalization of Constantinople'. Balfour thought that Wilson ought to know about the secret treaties, which characteristically he had failed to bring with him. A packet was hastily sent from London, which Balfour passed on to the president on 18 May. Wilson later denied all knowledge of the treaties, and Balfour could not remember what was in the parcel. It contained, in fact, the text of a statement by Balfour to the imperial war conference, emphasizing that 'the practical destruction of the Turkish Empire was one of the objects desired by the British government'; two copies of the Treaty of London; the so-called Sykes-Picot agreement regarding Asia Minor and ascribed to May 1916 (in other words, the agreement as modified by Russian participation); the exchange of letters with Russia in March–April 1915 concerning Constantinople and the Straits; and the Treaty of Bucharest with Rumania. Wilson never acknowledged receipt of this curious collection. In January 1918 Balfour wrote to Wilson about the secret treaties, adding cheerfully: 'it is not probable Italy will prolong the war in order to obtain her Adriatic claims'. Wilson ignored all these communications. His only war aim was the defeat of Germany, and he intended that the Allies should make peace on their own terms, which he would then endorse if they were sufficiently enlightened. Apart from the 'internationalization' of Constantinople, his only indication was to express to the French his approval of a 'scientific' peace, which would not reproduce 'the enormity committed by the Germans when they took Alsace-Lorraine from France'. This might be an endorsement of France's principal war aim; equally it might be a warning against it.

During the summer of 1917 the British and French Governments were pushed farther towards definition by the idealistic wind blowing from Russia. On 5 June the French chamber of deputies passed a 'peace resolution', demanding the return of Alsace-Lorraine, 'together with liberation of invaded territories and just reparation for damage'. Further, there must be 'durable guarantees for peace and independence for peoples great and small, in a league of nations such as has already been foreshadowed'. The senate passed a similar resolution, but omitted the reference to a League of Nations. The French Socialists wished to postulate a plebiscite even for Alsace-Lorraine. When this was refused, they withdrew from the government in September.

On 29 June Lloyd George had a shot at war aims in a speech at Glasgow. He dwelt at length on reparation for Belgium; gave one sentence to Serbia, three paragraphs to Mesopotamia, and one paragraph to the German colonies. The peroration of his speech demanded 'the democratization of the German government'. There was nothing about the League of Nations nor about the dismemberment of Austria-Hungary—not even a mention of Alsace-Lorraine. A month later, on 30 July, Balfour, the foreign secretary, was a little more precise in the House of Commons. Though he would not discuss 'how you are going to deal with such a great and ancient monarchy as Austria', he said: 'what we desire, of course, is that the nationalities composing that hetero-geneous State should be allowed to develop on their own lines'. He also expressed his 'own opinion, which is that, while France fights for Alsace and Lorraine, we should support her'. It was Kühlmann, the German secretary of state, not Balfour, who finally provoked Lloyd George into formally endorsing France's claim. Kühlmann implied in the Reichstag that the British would make peace without thought of Alsace and Lorraine, if Germany restored Belgium. On 11 October Lloyd George replied: 'However long the war may last, this country intends to stand by her gallant ally, France, until she redeems her oppressed children from the degradation of a foreign yoke.' It had taken more than three years of war to turn Alsace-Lorraine into a British war aim.

The shape of the war changed fundamentally in its last year. Russia had ceased to fight and soon made a separate peace. Italy was exhausted, France hardly less so. The British had to increase their contribution in ideas as well as in men if they were to hold their own with the United States. The collapse of Russia was not an unmixed disaster. The agreement over Constantinople could be forgotten; the sacred principle of internationalizing the Straits could be proclaimed—with American approval. Moreover, Poland could be resurrected, after being jettisoned by France the previous March. On 27 December Pichon, foreign minister under Clemenceau, said of Poland: 'We do not separate her cause from ours . . . we want her one, independent, indivisible.' The British did not share this enthusiasm for Poland. Indeed, in December 1917, Smuts, negotiating in Switzerland with an Austrian representative, suggested that Poland, together with Rumania and Serbia, should unite in a federation under the Habsburg emperor.

This, of course, was not official British policy. Balfour clearly disapproved of it. Once the chief opponent of the national principle in Ireland, he now backed it elsewhere and no doubt enjoyed overbidding the former Radicalism of his prime minister. Speaking in the house of commons on 6 November, he emphasized the recovery of Alsace-Lorraine and the liberation of Armenia and Poland as idealistic war aims—Armenia a particularly shrewd stroke at the Gladstonian tradition. These were casual hints. Lloyd George devised a more elaborate programme. He was in competition both with the Bolsheviks and with Wilson: Lansdowne's 'peace letter' of 29 November 1917, urging a *status quo* peace in return for the liberation of Belgium, was a further challenge to him. He secured the approval of Asquith and Grey, the principal leaders of the Liberal Opposition, and on 5 January 1918 gave at the trade union congress the most precise definition of British war aims. There were two clear negatives. 'The break-up of Austria-Hungary is no part of our war aims. . . . Nor are we fighting to deprive Turkey of its capital or of the rich and renowned lands of Asia Minor and Thrace, which are predominantly Turkish in race.' The secret treaty of March 1915 was safely forgotten, the agreement with Italy hardly less so.

On the positive side, 'the first requirement' was the complete restoration of Belgian independence and reparation for her devastation. In this the British Government had not wavered since the beginning of the war. Lloyd George added, less justifiably, that this was also the first requirement of the Allies. Next came the restoration of Serbia, Montenegro and the occupied parts of France, Italy and Rumania; and 'we mean to stand by the French Democracy to the death in the demand they make for reconsideration of the great wrong of 1871'. Lloyd George then dwelt at length on the dangers of a separate peace between Russia and Germany. He added as an afterthought the single sentence: 'We believe that an independent Poland, comprising all those genuinely Polish elements who desire to form part of it is an urgent necessity for the stability of Western Europe.' He endorsed two other national claims: 'the satisfaction of the legitimate claims of the Italians for union with those of their own race and tongue'; and 'that justice be done to men of Roumanian blood and speech in their legitimate aspirations'. Neither the Czechoslovaks nor the Yugoslavs were mentioned. Outside Europe the Straits were to be 'internationalized and neutralized', and 'Arabia, Armenia, Mesopotamia, Syria and Palestine are in our judgement entitled to a recognition of their separate national condition'. The secret treaties were tactfully repudiated: 'new circumstances have changed the conditions under which those arrangements were made'.

Lloyd George turned with obvious relief from these topics to the German colonies, which 'by the general principle of national self-determination' were never to return to Germany. He ended with a reference to the economic and other problems that would follow the war; but all he had to contribute to solving them was the single sentence: 'a great attempt must be made to establish by some international organization an alternative to war as a means of settling international disputes'. This would 'limit the burden of armaments and diminish the probability of war'. There was no reference to the German navy—a curious omission. Clearly Lloyd George felt committed to Belgium and to the French demand for Alsace-Lorraine. He honoured the Sykes-Picot agreement but disregarded the Treaty of London (or regarded it as synonymous with Italy's national claims—which it was not) and gave no thought to the agreement of St. Jean de Maurienne. Indeed 'the maintenance of the Turkish empire in the home lands of the Turkish race' was a direct repudiation of it. Italy had suffered the disaster of Caporetto since the agreement was made, and no doubt Lloyd George thought that she was lucky to remain in the war at all.

Lloyd George's programme was endorsed by Clemenceau in a single sentence on 6 January. The other allies did not express an opinion. This programme just managed to anticipate President Wilson's. He had earlier sought an agreed statement by the Allies, and House, his confidential adviser, spent the autumn of 1917 in Europe for this purpose. He failed, and Wilson therefore decided to act on his own. The final spur was the prospect of a separate peace between Germany and Russia, which Wilson hoped to prevent by an idealistic statement. On 8 January he announced the Fourteen Points to congress. These partly—but only partly—coincided with Lloyd George's programme, though they had been drafted independently. There were four general propositions: 'open covenants of peace, openly arrived at'; 'absolute freedom of navigation upon the seas'; 'the removal, so far as possible, of all economic barriers'; and 'adequate guarantees given and taken that national armaments will be

reduced'. There was to be 'a free, open-minded, and absolutely impartial adjustment of all colonial claims'. All
Russian territory must be evacuated.

Then came the practical terms. 'Belgium must be evacuated and restored.' 'All French territory should be freed and
the invaded portions restored, and the wrong done to France
by Prussia in 1871 in the matter of Alsace-Lorraine . . .
should be righted.' The clause concerning Italy was carefully
designed to supersede the Treaty of London: 'a readjustment
of the frontiers of Italy should be effected along clearly
recognizable lines of nationality'. The claims of the Czecho-
slovaks were also repudiated: 'the peoples of Austria-Hungary . . . should be accorded the freest opportunity of
autonomous development'. Though Rumania, Serbia and
Montenegro were to be evacuated and restored, there was no
hint that any of them should receive any acquisition of territory. Nor was it clear that the Ottoman empire was to be
dismembered. The non-Turkish nationalities were merely
offered 'an undoubted security of life and an absolutely
unmolested opportunity of autonomous development'. The
Dardanelles were to be permanently opened under international guarantees—the Bosphorus was apparently forgotten. The pledge to Poland was a good deal more specific
than any given by a British or French statesman: 'an independent Polish state . . . which should include the territories
inhabited by indisputably Polish populations, which should
be assured a free and secure access to the sea, and whose
political and economic independence and territorial integrity
should be guaranteed by international covenant'. The final
point defined the future League of Nations: 'a general association . . . for the purpose of affording mutual guarantees of
political independence and territorial integrity to great and
small States alike'. There was one most striking omission.
No word of the Fourteen Points referred to the democratization of the German Government.

The Fourteen Points contained nothing that Wilson had
not said before. But previously he had expressed academic
approval of aims which the Entente were to realize; now

he made them his own. 'The program of the world's peace is our program; and that program, the only possible program, as we see it, is this.' Lloyd George virtually endorsed the Fourteen Points on 18 January: 'President Wilson and myself laid down what was substantially the same programme of demands for the termination of the war', though he expressed some doubt about the freedom of the seas. None of the other Allies made any public statement. The Italian government contemplated a protest, but thought better of it. The Serb minister at Washington said privately that ignoring his country was 'the absolute bankruptcy of Allied policy'.

Wilson laid down further general propositions in later speeches. None of them added to his practical programme except the principle stated on 4 July: 'the destruction of every arbitrary power anywhere that can separately, secretly, and of its single choice disturb the peace of the world'. It was on the basis of this clause that Wilson demanded assurance that Germany had become a democratic country, when the Germans sought an armistice in October. There was a more important change of policy in the last months of the war: the Allies jettisoned Austria-Hungary. The attempts at a separate peace with her had broken down. What is more, the Italians, in their desperate condition, grasped at any assistance and in April 1918 organized a congress of oppressed nationalities at Rome, where they sat side by side with Yugoslavs, whom they hoped shortly to oppress. The real gainers were the Czechoslovaks, whose claims the Italians could back unreservedly without risk to themselves. The Allies had, too, the example of Russian Bolshevism before their eyes. They feared similar developments in central Europe when the Habsburg monarchy broke up, and nothing did more to endear the principle of national self-determination to them than the anti-Bolshevik achievements of the Czech legion in Siberia.

At the end of May an Entente conference met at Versailles intending to launch a grandiose programme of national liberation, but it broke against Italian reluctance to recognize Yugoslavia even now. On 3 June it declared in favour of 'a

united and independent Poland with free access to the sea'
and expressed 'lively sympathy for the Czechoslovak and
Jugoslav people'. Beneš, who was conducting Czechoslovak
affairs in Europe, decided that he could not be held back any
longer by the Yugoslavs. He went ahead and obtained recognition on his own. On 28 June France recognized the Czechoslovak National Council as 'supreme organ of the nation, and
the first basis of a future Czechoslovak government'. On 9
August Great Britain accepted the Czechoslovaks 'as an
Allied nation' and recognized the National Council 'as the
present trustee of the future Czechoslovak Government'.
On 2 September the United States outbid the Allies and
recognized the National Council 'as a *de facto* belligerent
government'. Czechoslovakia was thus legally in existence
before the end of the war. Poland got a more grudging
acknowledgement in October, Yugoslavia none.

In October the Central Powers were defeated and sought
peace negotiations on the basis of the Fourteen Points and
Wilson's 'subsequent pronouncements'. Wilson made it clear
that the programme of national autonomy had been made out
of date by later events. In any case the armistices with Bulgaria, Austria-Hungary, and Turkey were concluded on a
purely military basis without reference to the Fourteen
Points or any other political programme. The Germans were,
however, informed on 5 November that the Allied governments were willing to make peace on the terms of the Fourteen Points and the principles enunciated in Wilson's subsequent addresses. They made two reservations: one—directed
more against the United States than against Germany—concerning the freedom of the seas; the other that 'compensation
will be made by Germany for all damage done to the civilian
population of the Allies and their property by the aggression
of Germany by land, by sea and from the air'.

One final gloss was added to Allied war aims before the
peace conference met at Paris. Clemenceau and Foch came
to London on a triumphal visit from 30 November to 3
December. They wished to secure British backing for their
claim to the Saar and their plan for a separate Rhineland,

which had been endorsed by Russia in the far-off happy days of February 1917. They did not succeed. Lloyd George refused to create 'a new Alsace-Lorraine in Europe'. Nevertheless Clemenceau held out a tempting bait. He would agree that Palestine should become a British, instead of an international, mandate, and he would transfer Mosul—with its oilfields—from the French to the British sphere. Lloyd George accepted this 'verbal agreement'. What did he give 'verbally' in return? According to his own account, nothing. Not only did he reject Foch's scheme for the Rhineland: he asserted at the Supreme Council on 20 March 1919 that even the Sykes-Picot agreement had been superseded by an Anglo-French statement of 7 November 1918, which promised 'to encourage and help the establishment of native governments and administrations in Syria and Mesopotamia'. On the other hand, Tardieu, one of Clemenceau's associates, said in the French chamber that Clemenceau had yielded over Mosul and Palestine 'because he needed both general agreement with Great Britain and her local support in Syria'; and he described Clemenceau's price as 'total support given by England to the French plans in case of American objections'. Clemenceau certainly kept his bargain. Perhaps Lloyd George did also. Not only did Syria become a French mandate after some British objections: France got the Saar for fifteen years and an occupation of the Rhineland which Clemenceau intended should be permanent.

For the rest, Alsace-Lorraine returned to France. Belgium was liberated. Poland and Czechoslovakia became independent national states. The Rumanians got more than they deserved, though less than they demanded; the Yugoslavs less than they deserved, but more than they hoped for. Russian ambitions were swamped in the storm of the Bolshevik Revolution. Italy did not make the gains which she had been promised in the Treaty of London. She had been the most calculating and the most grasping of the Allies, and was consequently the more disappointed in a peace settlement where ideal principles counted for much more than 'the secret treaties'.

IX

LLOYD GEORGE: RISE AND FALL

Leslie Stephen Lecture, 1961

ON 7 December 1916 Lloyd George had a busy day. In the evening he returned to his room at the war office with his devoted adherent, Dr. Christopher Addison. The building was empty. A solitary messenger produced a cold chicken— what strange things they kept at the war office; warmed up some soup and a bit of fish; Lloyd George unearthed a bottle of champagne. This scratch supper celebrated the triumph of 'the people'. It was Lloyd George's first meal as prime minister. Years afterwards he wrote: 'There had never before been a "ranker" raised to the premiership— certainly not one except Disraeli who had not passed through the Staff College of the old Universities.'[1] Like many of Lloyd George's best remarks, this is not strictly accurate. The Duke of Wellington did not go to a university. The rule has often been broken since. With Lloyd George's successors, the old universities have scored a draw—four all. Yet essentially Lloyd George's remark was true. No other premier has been a 'ranker' to the same extent. Even Ramsay Mac-Donald took on the colour of his surroundings despite his origins—perhaps too much so. Lloyd George remained the great 'rogue' of British political life in more senses than one.

Lloyd George was not marked out only by having escaped the staff college of the old universities. He was an exception

[1] Lloyd George, *War Memoirs,* i. 621.

among British prime ministers in almost every way—in
nationality, in economic origin, in religion, in profession. He
was Welsh; he was born in a poor family; he was a Nonconformist; he was a solicitor until politics absorbed him.
He was the only prime minister with a native tongue other
than English—perhaps I should say as well as English; the
only one with a sense of national oppression or at any rate
inequality. He was much poorer at the start than any future
prime minister except Ramsay MacDonald, and, unlike Mac-
Donald, he did not marry a rich wife. He was the only prime
minister except Neville Chamberlain who was a practising
Nonconformist when in office,[1] though his religious outlook
does not seem to have been orthodox—it was a sort of
pantheism of the people, combined with pleasure in the sing-
ing of Baptist hymns. He was the only solicitor to become
prime minister, and this, though it seems less significant, had
its influence also. Solicitors are, by definition, the 'O.R.s'
of the legal profession. Barristers like the ringing phrase and
the drama of open dispute. Solicitors prefer to settle behind
the scenes.

How did this ranker attain supreme power? And how,
having succeeded, did he come to lose it? These are questions
of endless fascination, whether considered in terms of the
individual man or as an exercise in political history. The first
question—how he got there—has been much discussed. Indeed there are few political episodes which have been canvassed in greater detail. But even the incomparable dissec-
tion by Lord Beaverbrook, which will be read as long as men
are interested in political tactics, leaves much unsaid. The
accounts of this affair start off, as it were, with the great topic
settled: Lloyd George is clearly the man who will win the
war. They deal with the mechanics of how he got to the top
when his reputation was made; they do not explain how so

---

[1] Asquith, though of Nonconformist origin, had ceased to have any
open Nonconformist allegiance by the time he became prime minister.
The other non-Anglican prime ministers, of whom there have been
several, were Scottish Presbyterians and therefore conformists in their
own country.

many people reached agreement on this reputation, or exactly what it rested on. The second question has been more casually treated. Lloyd George himself was perhaps bewildered that he had fallen, others bewildered that they had ever put him into a position from which to fall. Who, having fallen out of love, can explain why he was ever in, let alone how he got out of it again? These are my two themes —the rise to power, and the fall from it; two different aspects of the same baffling personality.

Lloyd George was a politician from first to last and nothing else, though he sometimes made claim to distinction as a journalist, as an author, and—perhaps with more justification—as a nursery-gardener. He did not come late into national politics with his reputation already established elsewhere, as some other outsiders have done—Joseph Chamberlain for example. He became a member of parliament at the age of twenty-seven, and he achieved a record for uninterrupted representation of the same constituency which no other prime minister can equal or nearly approach. He lived only for politics. He talked politics in his leisure hours —either the politics of the moment, or political reminiscence. Political history was his only serious reading. He found diversion in cheap thrillers. His favourite bedtime author was Ridgwell Cullum. He had no taste in art or music, no knowledge of contemporary literature, no interest in the affairs of the mind outside the political world. I doubt whether he understood economic principles, though he was quick to turn them to advantage.

Though Lloyd George spent his life among politicians and in parliament, he cared little for either of them. He was never intimate with established politicians of the ordinary kind, and he did not frequent the recognized social centres. His associates were men outside the conventional pattern like himself: Churchill, the grandson of a duke, who crossed the floor to become a Radical; Rufus Isaacs, son of a fruit merchant who rose to be an earl, lord chief justice, and viceroy of India; F. E. Smith—the smith of his own fortunes—who invented a youth of extreme poverty for himself and perhaps came to believe in it. Even with them Lloyd George was reserved. Only Churchill called him 'David'; for all others he was 'L.G.' He stood out against the growing use of Christian names: 'I am not very active in that way. I don't believe in being too familiar with people.'[1] Similarly, he took little trouble to sound parliamentary feeling outside the debating chamber. He rarely appeared in the smoking-room. He knew few members by sight and, before becoming prime minister in 1916, had to entrust Christopher Addison with the task of discovering which Liberal members would support him. He relinquished the leadership of the House to Bonar Law with relief and thereafter never made a speech as prime minister without complaining that the House was distracting him from his real work. In later years, after his fall from power, he held court in his private room and did not welcome stray visitors.

Coming into the British system from outside, he had no respect for its traditions or accepted formalities. As prime minister, he failed to sustain the elaborate shadow-play which treats the monarch as something more than a figure-head. He promised peerages without first securing royal approval. He appointed ministers and then informed the king by telephone. He detested titles. This, no doubt, is why he distributed them so lavishly. If others were fools enough to buy, he was willing to sell. It gave added zest to his campaign against landowners that the greatest of them were dukes, and he would have derived less pleasure from humiliating Curzon, if Curzon had not been a marquess (of Lloyd George's creation) and for ever parading pride of birth. Most of all, he distrusted the permanent officials. Sometimes he overrode them. He is said to have been the only minister of modern times who could defeat the obstinacy even of treasury officials. Usually, however, he preferred to circumvent them. He carried his private secretaries with him from one department to another, much as a French politician does, culminating, when he was prime minister, in the creation of a duplicate civil service dependent on himself, the 'Garden

[1] Riddell, *Intimate Diary*, p. 287.

Suburb'.[1] After the war, Philip Kerr, one of this 'suburb', was more influential in foreign affairs than Lord Curzon, the foreign secretary; just as J. T. Davies, Lloyd George's principal private secretary, was a more important figure than the permanent head of the civil service.

Lloyd George never hesitated to go behind the backs of his established advisers, listening to amateur advice and then forming his opinion with little regard to the official papers. He consulted junior officers back from France, including his own son, for arguments to use against Haig, the commander-in-chief, and Robertson, chief of the imperial general staff. He got Lieutenant-Commander Kenworthy to brief him against the Lords of the Admiralty. Kenworthy was smuggled into No. 10 Downing Street late at night by Northcliffe through the garden door. The most striking instance of Lloyd George's unconventional methods is the origin of the National Health service—that revolutionary contribution to modern life. One can imagine how it would have begun in the ordinary way: a royal commission, long papers from experts, an accumulation of facts and figures. Lloyd George merely sent W. J. Braithwaite, a junior official in the treasury, to find how Bismarck's system of insurance worked in Germany. Braithwaite toured Germany and then travelled overnight to the south of France. On 3 January 1911 he caught up with Lloyd George at Nice. Lloyd George, accompanied by some friends, took him to the pier; set out chairs not too near the band; ordered drinks; and said: 'Now tell us all about it.' Braithwaite discoursed for four hours. When he had finished, the Welfare State had been born. A symbol of Lloyd George

---

[1] Lloyd George introduced two other French innovations into British political life. Until 1915 British ministers were secretaries, first lords, presidents of boards. The first avowed minister was the minister of munitions, Lloyd George himself; he soon created others. Again, British ministers with nothing to do were given a sinecure. They were not ministers without portfolio—strictly speaking, no British minister has a portfolio, he has seals or a royal warrant. The first minister without portfolio, Lansdowne, was appointed in 1915 on Lloyd George's suggestion; and the list was soon full of them. Perhaps Lloyd George's casual attitude to his private finances was also learnt from France, or perhaps it was natural to a Welshman.

indeed—the pier at Nice, the band, the hastily improvised explanation, and then the gigantic results. It gives added point to the story that there is no pier at Nice; perhaps there was one then.

Lloyd George rarely showed loyalty to those who broke ranks to work with him. J. T. Davies was rewarded by being made a director of the Suez Canal Company. Others were less fortunate. Braithwaite created the National Health system almost single-handed under Lloyd George's inspiration. As soon as it was made, Lloyd George deposited him in the obscurity of a special commissioner of income tax. They met again only once, twenty years later. Lloyd George said: 'Hello, Braithwaite, what have you been doing all this time?' Braithwaite replied: 'My duty I hope, sir, where I was sent to do it.' Politicians who worked with Lloyd George were treated in the same way. Christopher Addison had a large share in making Lloyd George prime minister. Some years later, when Addison's lavish expenditure on housing— incurred on Lloyd George's prompting—aroused Unionist hostility, Lloyd George jettisoned him without warning, and apologized to the house that loyalty to an old friend had led him to keep an incompetent minister in office. For Lloyd George, no ties were sacred. Churchill stood solidly by Lloyd George during the Marconi scandal in 1913. Lloyd George did not repay the debt when Churchill ran into trouble over the expedition to the Dardanelles. He said, quite untruly: 'Churchill is the man who brought Turkey into the war againt us', and let the Unionists drive Churchill from office. Lloyd George was fond of saying: 'There is no friendship at the top.' It was certainly true in his case.

Lloyd George did not rely on individuals, however eminent. He recognized no intermediaries between himself and 'the people'. His relations with the House of Commons were a mixture of uneasy mastery and distrust. His set pieces in parliament were not remarkable. His long speech introducing the People's Budget of 1909 was poorly delivered, and one listener surmised that Lloyd George himself did not understand what he was saying. It was different when he was answering criticism or silencing opposition by last-minute concessions. He met objections to the National Health scheme so skilfully, and with such moderation, that in the end most Unionists voted for it. As prime minister, he never allowed his opponents to get the issue clear and always raised some unexpected red herring which left them baffled. So, when accused of weakness towards Germany during the peace negotiations of 1919, he rode off with an irrelevant attack on Lord Northcliffe, which delighted even his strongest critics. His greatest triumph came in the Maurice debate of May 1918. Asquith, who launched it, was universally described as the greatest parliamentarian, and he had a good case; but no novice was more catastrophically out-manœuvred. Lloyd George summed up the debate afterwards: 'They have gone away saying—we have caught the little beggar out speaking the truth for once.' Whether he was speaking the truth on that occasion, no one has been able to decide from that day to this.

For Lloyd George, parliament was less important than the public meeting. He said: 'My platform is the country.' This was the time when all political leaders did a great deal of public speaking. The period opened in the 1880s, after Gladstone's Midlothian campaigns; it tailed off in the 1930s, perhaps because interest in politics declined, perhaps because of the radio. Lloyd George came just at the top of the wave. His style was all his own. Other statesmen spoke in formal terms, carefully prepared. Churchill, for instance, learnt his early speeches, word for word, by heart and read his later ones. Lloyd George spoke with his audience, not to them, and snapped up phrases as they were thrown at him. 'Ninepence for fourpence' was the result of one such interruption; making Germany pay to the uttermost farthing, the less happy result of another. Most public speakers seemed to be the contemporaries of Henry Irving or Beerbohm Tree. Lloyd George gave a music-hall turn, worthy of Harry Lauder or George Robey, the prime minister of mirth; and the great days of the music hall, roughly from 1900 to 1930, corresponded exactly with his. In 1923 Lloyd George was persuaded to use a

E

microphone for the first time, and he accepted it ever
afterwards. I suspect that it ruined his public style, as it
certainly ruined the music hall.

Speechmaking was not Lloyd George's only instrument
for projecting himself on the country, perhaps not even
the most important. No public man has made more use of the
press. This was not new. Palmerston wrote leaders for the
Globe and the *Morning Chronicle*, often reproducing the very
words of his dispatches and rewarding the proprietor of the
latter with a baronetcy. Salisbury wrote in the *Standard*,
and made his ghost, Alfred Austin, Poet Laureate. Even Sir
Edward Grey briefed J. A. Spender, of the *Westminster
Gazette*. Lloyd George approached the press in a different
way. He was never forthcoming to reporters. On the contrary
he was the first prime minister who employed a press
secretary to keep them at bay, and even then often complained
of their misrepresentations. Lloyd George went for the man
at the top—the editor and, still more, the proprietor. Why
bother to make a case when the proprietor could make it more
decisively simply by issuing an order? The most famous example came in 1918. Lloyd George, angered that the *Daily
Chronicle* had enlisted his critic, Frederick Maurice, as military
correspondent, got a group of Coalition Liberals to buy the
paper and turned out the editor, Robert Donald, at twenty-
four hours' notice.[1] This was not his first exercise in financial
influence. As early as 1900 he persuaded George Cadbury to
buy the *Daily News* and to turn it overnight from a pro-war
to a pro-Boer paper. Usually he used less direct means. Common sympathy with the Boers established a deep intimacy
between Lloyd George and C. P. Scott, owner-editor of the
Manchester Guardian, an intimacy not really broken even when
Scott was denouncing the behaviour of the Black and Tans in
Ireland. Scott remained faithful even unto death: almost his
last act was to swing the *Manchester Guardian* against the
National government, and behind Lloyd George, during the

[1] This manipulation of 'public opinion' proved useful to Lloyd George
in another way. He put some of his private political fund into the *Daily
Chronicle*, and sold out in 1926 at a fourfold profit.

financial crisis of 1931. Even more important for Lloyd George was his friendship with Sir William Robertson Nicoll, editor of the *British Weekly*, a man now forgotten, but wielding decisive power in his time. It is hardly too much to say that Robertson Nicoll was the man who first, by supporting Lloyd George, raised him up; and then, by withdrawing his support, cast him down.

Newspaper proprietors in the stricter sense were flattered by Lloyd George and often ennobled by him: Riddell, owner of the *News of the World*, the first divorced person to be made a peer; Rothermere; Beaverbrook. Lloyd George had a curious on-and-off relationship with Northcliffe, the greatest of them all, intimate at one moment, hostile at the next. The two men had much in common, despite their conflicts, both sprung from the people, both impatient with conventional politicians. There was in both the same mixture of impulsiveness and calculation, though Northcliffe was the less calculating of the two. When once asked to cooperate with Northcliffe, Lloyd George replied: 'I would as soon go for a walk round Walton Heath with a grasshopper.' A good analogy; but who more like a grasshopper than Lloyd George himself? Lloyd George did not court the newspaper proprietors merely as the makers of public opinion. He genuinely believed that they understood this opinion and could interpret it. How else had they achieved their enormous circulations? Hence he canvassed their advice before taking decisive action. He supposed also that they possessed executive ability of the highest order. When he filled his administration with 'press lords', this was not only to 'buy' them; he thought that the work would be done better by them than by anyone else, and it often was. Then, by an odd twist, he discovered the same abilities in himself. After all, if the inarticulate Northcliffe and the ponderous Rothermere had journalistic genius, how much more must Lloyd George have it too. I doubt if this were the case. Though he was highly paid by American papers after he ceased to be prime minister, this was rather for his name than for the quality of his contributions. But Lloyd George believed himself suited to a great journalistic post. In 1922 it was seriously proposed that a group of wealthy friends should buy *The Times*, then being hawked around after Northcliffe's death, and set him up as editor. Lloyd George was ready, eager, to resign the premiership for this purpose. No doubt he had other reasons for wishing to be rid of office. Nevertheless the affair is striking testimony that Lloyd George rated the world of journalism highly, perhaps even more highly than the world of politics. Editors of *The Times* have often believed that they were more important than prime ministers. Lloyd George was the only prime minister who apparently agreed with them.

Parliament, platform, press, one element needs to be fitted into place, maybe the key place: politics. Though Lloyd George was never a good party man, indifferent to many party doctrines and regardless of party discipline, he was first returned as a Liberal, and managed to call himself a Liberal of some sort or another throughout his political life. The peculiar circumstances of the Liberal party gave him his opportunity; later snatched it away again.

Few writers have noticed how peculiar these circumstances were. Historians of recent times assume, perhaps rightly, that the two-party system is a permanent feature of British politics; and they go on to assume, with less justification, that the swing of the pendulum follows inevitably from this. Hence they find nothing surprising in the Liberal victory of 1906. On the contrary, it was against all the rules. When Lloyd George entered parliament in 1890, the Liberal party seemed clearly on the way out: sustained by Gladstone's great name, but then doomed to decline and disintegration. So it happened: defeat in 1895, and thereafter disruption into warring factions. This was not surprising. Historic liberalism was a *bourgeois* cause, inspired by the advance of *laissez-faire* capitalism and successful in the days of limited suffrage. It lost drive as individual enterprise diminished and it offered little which could attract a mass electorate. This was the common pattern all over Europe. The National Liberal party in Germany, the Liberal party in Austria, the French opportunists, the moderate Italian Liberals who followed

Cavour, all saw their greatness disappear. Oldfashioned British liberalism really ended in 1874, as Gladstone recognized by resigning from the leadership. The party was revived only by the freak controversies first over the Eastern Question and then over Home Rule. But Home Rule could not keep it going permanently, particularly when most Liberals were not interested in it.

How, then, did British liberalism come to have its greatest success in the early twentieth century, when—on any rational calculation—it should have been dead? The answer is to be found in economic developments which also went against the rules. Individualistic capitalism had a second innings, a sort of deathbed repentance. It is rather like the Solent which, owing to the bottleneck in the Channel between Cherbourg and St. Catherine's Point, has four tides a day. You are just resigning yourself to a desolate stretch of sand or pebble when the tide comes flooding in again. So it was with British economy, and for a paradoxical reason. The terms of trade, which in the later nineteenth century had been moving in favour of Great Britain, at the end of the century turned against her. As all Europe and much of the United States became industrialized, the cost of raw materials went up; so did the price of foodstuffs which everyone was importing. There was increased social discontent in Great Britain, as real wages declined—a social discontent which Lloyd George did much to exploit; there was increased hostility to the 'stomach taxes' which Tariff Reform involved. There was something else: a renewed demand for the products of the old British staples—coal, shipbuilding, textiles; staples which had been losing their preeminence. Suddenly, with the increased prosperity of producers of raw materials outside Europe, they boomed again. All three surpassed their previous records, and British exports, thanks mainly to the old staples, reached their all-time peak in 1913.

Instead of undertaking a new industrial revolution, Great Britain could prosper again in the old centres of industry in the old way. This unexpected revival brought with it a second edition of new men, self-reliant, self-made, impatiently

Radical, far removed from the intellectual refinement of the established Liberal leaders. They were more assertive than their predecessors of fifty years before, unawed by the prestige of the conventional system. Cobden, for instance, despaired of ever attaining real power. His lesser successors had no such doubts. Here is a significant indication. Like their predecessors, the new men were mostly Dissenters, at any rate in upbringing, though—like Lloyd George—most of them did not take their religious allegiance at all precisely. They were Dissenters with a difference. The nineteenth-century Dissenters called themselves Nonconformists— recognition that they were a tolerated minority. Early in the twentieth century they changed their official description and became the Free Churches—assertion of equality, perhaps even of superior virtue. The Dissenters swarmed into the parliament of 1906. As Halévy pointed out long ago, that parliament had more non-Anglicans in it than any since the time of Oliver Cromwell. Barebones had come again.

These new men were the making of Lloyd George. The very things which distinguished him from other Liberal leaders brought him close to the self-made businessmen. He had no university education; nor had they. He was of poor origin; so were they. Above all, he was an avowed Free Churchman, and this became the symbol of his unique position. This first picked him out from the Liberal back-benchers and made him a national figure. It started with the Boer war. The Boers were regarded, rather perversely, as champions of the small man against the encroachments of the City and monopoly finance. Moreover they were Free Churchmen, or something like it. There would have been much less pro-Boer enthusiasm in Great Britain if the Boers had been Roman Catholics. It was an added advantage to Lloyd George that most Liberal leaders supported the Boer war almost as heartily as Unionist ministers did. Still, this was a passing phase. What really made Lloyd George's standing was the controversy over the Education Bill of 1902. Here again many Liberal leaders—influenced by the Fabians and friendly to Morant, its author—favoured the Bill. Lloyd

George fought it virtually alone. When the political argument shifted from Education to Free Trade, he lost his preeminence. He never cared much for Free Trade, nor understood the topics in dispute. Others took up the running. Asquith, always strongest in negation, eclipsed him. Nevertheless, thanks to the earlier conflicts, Lloyd George had forced his way to the front and established his claim to high office.

Lloyd George was the outstanding 'new' Radical in the Liberal government of 1905. Office gave him the opportunity to show his great executive capacity—his unrivalled ability for getting things done. The things he did were all his own, things not envisaged by ordinary liberalism or by the party programme. Everyone knows the rather synthetic passions which he aroused over the People's Budget of 1909. Yet curiously he was the least involved in the subsequent controversy over the House of Lords. He knew instinctively that the people—his sort of people—were not deeply stirred by the constitutional intricacies which fascinated Liberal lawyers. His judgement was correct. The two general elections of 1910, and particularly the second, produced more excitement among candidates and less among the electors than perhaps any others of modern times. Lloyd George showed his real opinion of the affair by quietly devising the National Health scheme, and carrying it, when the constitutional storm was blowing its hardest. Indeed, he proposed to settle all the burning issues between the parties—dead issues in his opinion—by agreement. He tried quite sincerely to promote a Coalition government; less sincerely perhaps even at the price of his own withdrawal. What he really wanted was 'a government of businessmen'—a revealing phrase—in other words of Radical backbenchers.

Lloyd George had something else in common with the new men. His financial position was improving like theirs. The private finances of public men are rarely touched on by their biographers. Still, it is pretty clear that most public men have been the poorer for their life of service, particularly when they held office. Lloyd George was in debt when he became

president of the board of trade in 1905; his position was very
different when he ceased to be prime minister in 1922. He
was the first prime minister since Walpole to leave office
markedly richer than he entered it. This is not all mystery.
Wealthy admirers entertained and endowed him. Riddell
gave him a house at Walton Heath—burnt by suffragettes
during the building—which he later sold at a good price;
Andrew Carnegie bequeathed him an annuity of £2,000, in
remote applause for his democratic achievements. But most
of his success defies inquiry. Though Lloyd George became
well-off, he did not acquire a country-house near London
until after the war. Disliking life in London, he went off,
whenever he could, to a luxury hotel at Brighton or the
south of France, with an accompanying flock of civil servants
and political adherents, all presumably paid for by the
treasury. It did not occur to him that he was cutting himself
off from 'the people' by living in this way. 'The people'
whom he knew, the Free Church Radicals, lived in exactly
the same way.

Besides, he remained closer to the people than any other
Liberal minister including John Burns. Lloyd George was the
link between the Liberal government and Labour on its trade-
union side. Trade unions have now become an accepted,
indeed an essential, part of the social order. It is hard to
think back to a time, only fifty years ago, when unions
were not recognized in many leading industries, when
working-men were held to be 'not like us', and when it could
be solemnly asserted that miners would keep coal in the bath
if they were given bathrooms. Labour was asserting its
independence in the early twentieth century, and the Liberal
government were repeatedly drawn into trade disputes. Their
mediation was still embarrassed and aloof. A minister thought
he had done well if he got masters and men—another
revealing phrase—into the same room. Lloyd George interpreted mediation differently. He was out to conciliate the
men, and he extracted concessions from the employers by any
means that occurred to him. It is tempting to surmise that he
made his Mansion House speech of 21 July 1911, stirring up

the Agadir crisis, so as to frighten the railway companies with the spectre of war into settling the great railway strike much in favour of the unions some three weeks later. At any rate, in the years before the war, Lloyd George was the favourite and most successful industrial mediator among ministers. He always got a settlement which enhanced his reputation at the same time.

The outbreak of war advanced Lloyd George's position in three ways. He was essential as the spokesman of the Radical Free Churches; he could display, still more, his great executive powers; he was the only minister who could handle Labour. The decision to go to war revolved round him. There would no doubt have been a majority for war in any case: the Unionists and the moderate Liberals would have supported it. But it seemed until the last moment that there might be also bitter opposition and opposition of the most dangerous kind, opposition on grounds of morality. It is a common opinion nowadays, and was a common opinion then, that wars are opposed for motives of class, that is by the working-class movement. Experience is quite other: opposition to war is effective and decisive only when sustained by moral principle, though it may be that the working-class is more moral than others. This was true in regard to the Boer war; it was true over the Suez affair; even, I think, true over the proposed war of intervention against Soviet Russia in 1920. That war was prevented because it was wicked, not because Soviet Russia was 'the workers' state'. So, too, in August 1914, the Free Churches, not the Labour movement, held the key position. When Lloyd George, sustained by Robertson Nicoll, came down on the side of war, he determined that there would be national unity, though, in a longer perspective, the two men sealed the death warrant of the Free Churches as a great moral force. His action mattered not only in August 1914; he was the principal guarantor of national unity as long as the war lasted, in a position—though he did not appreciate this for some time—to dictate his own terms.

The war also gave Lloyd George the opportunity to run things in the way he liked to run them. He could improvise;

E*

he could disregard precedent. Any other man would have quailed at starting a ministry of munitions from scratch. Lloyd George rejoiced that, when he entered the requisitioned hotel allotted to the new ministry, it contained a table, two chairs, many mirrors—and no civil servants. Alone among Liberal ministers, he appreciated that the war could not be conducted on the basis of *laissez-faire*. Perhaps he did not altogether deserve his reputation as the man who got things done. But at least he tried to get them done, which was more than could be said for anyone else in high office.

The third, and perhaps most important, asset came to Lloyd George unforeseen and by accident. It had hardly occurred to him that he would be the chief conciliator of Labour. Indeed it did not occur to him, or to anyone else, that in wartime the conciliation of Labour would be even more urgent than the raising of recruits. Until August 1914 the British people played a negative part in public life. Their only duties were to pay their taxes and not to cause trouble for the governing class. Suddenly their position changed. It was not enough to keep them quiet; they had to cooperate actively. Lloyd George was the chief instrument in industrial mobilization, thanks to his previous successes with the trade unions, and this even before he became minister of munitions. On 27 March 1915 he met the leaders of the engineering unions at the treasury: they agreed to drop restrictive practices for the duration, and received in return some rather vague promise of industrial partnership. This was a date of historic importance: the moment when the trade unions ceased to be merely instruments of resistance, and stepped, however half-heartedly, into a share of control. It was the most significant event in the history of British trade unions, and hence of the British working-class, since the repeal of the Combination Acts, and it was all Lloyd George's doing. He has left a vivid account of the scene—the union leaders leaning casually against a chair which Queen Anne was reputed to have used when she attended the Treasury Board, and A. J. Balfour, appropriate representative of the governing class, regarding them with tolerant surprise. Lloyd George writes: 'His ideas of government were inherited from the days when Queen Anne sat on that throne. . . . This scene was fundamentally different. He saw those stalwart artisans leaning against and sitting on the steps of the throne of the dead queen, and on equal terms negotiating conditions with the Government of the day. . . . Queen Anne was indeed dead. I felt that his detached and enquiring mind was bewildered by this sudden revelation of a new power and that he must take time to assimilate the experience.'[1] Lloyd George went further along the same path after he became minister of munitions. Though, strictly speaking, engineering alone was his concern, he acted as the unofficial minister for industry, called in whenever there were difficulties in the coalfields or the shipyards, and overriding the dogmatic follies of the minister technically responsible—Runciman, president of the board of trade. In this work of conciliation, Lloyd George established a partnership with Arthur Henderson—nominally president of the board of education, actually the representative of 'Labour' in the Coalition government. Henderson always preferred to play second fiddle, and he transferred to Lloyd George the support which he had previously given to MacDonald. The two men tackled industrial unrest together—not always successfully, but better than anyone else did.

Here then were Lloyd George's unique assets, assets which grew in strength as the war proceeded. Moreover the circumstances of the war made it easier for him to exploit these assets. Not only did 'the people' count for more; their voice became unexpectedly more effective. The Asquith coalition was a pact between the two front benches, a pact to avoid dispute and to keep things quiet. The press had to provide the criticism which was silenced in parliament; and practically all the press was on Lloyd George's side. It is often held that this was due to his personal intrigues. He is supposed to have 'nobbled' the press lords. I doubt whether anyone could 'nobble' Northcliffe. I am sure that no one could 'nobble' C. P. Scott, J. L. Garvin, Robert Donald, or

[1] Lloyd George, *War Memoirs*, i. 177.

Geoffrey Dawson. All these men passionately wanted Lloyd George as prime minister, and their united support is the most powerful evidence that he was the right man for the job. There was another factor. The backbenchers, both Unionist and Liberal, were increasingly restive at the silence which had been imposed upon them. They threatened to revolt, and this revolt brought Lloyd George to supreme power. In the crisis of December 1916, he had three kingmakers, none of them from the front bench. Max Aitken brought over Bonar Law, a backbencher in spirit, even though he was Unionist leader; Christopher Addison mobilized the backbench Radicals; Arthur Henderson delivered the solid backing of Labour, to his own surprise. There was one striking gap: the party Whips played no part at all. They were the instrument which broke in Asquith's hands.

Lloyd George was given two tasks as prime minister: a more energetic conduct of the war, and a closer partnership with the people. It was because Lloyd George enjoyed the confidence of 'the people' that the Unionist leaders came over to him, even though the revolt had been directed originally as much against them as against the frontbench Liberals. The Unionists had always been readier to make their peace with 'democracy' from the time of Disraeli onwards. The Liberals feared it and Asquith tried to fight the revolt entirely within the closed circle of the governing class. The Liberal leaders had a curious belief in their divine right to rule. Bewildered by their defeat, they grasped at the myth that Lloyd George had intrigued himself to the top and, by dint of repeating it, got others to believe it too. In reality, Asquith fought to retain power as much as Lloyd George fought to gain it, and his later complaints resemble those of an ageing heavyweight who has been knocked out by a younger, more agile, opponent. Nevertheless, Lloyd George paid a bitter price for victory. In Churchill's words, he had seized power, and the governing class never forgave him. Even the Unionist leaders who went with him meant to discard him once the emergency was over.

Lloyd George also suffered, in the long run, from the

backing which the press gave him. Members of parliament
like to regard themselves as the sole voice of the people and
see in the press a rival power, illegitimate and irresponsible. The house of commons has never forgiven its defeat
at the hands of John Wilkes, and there is no more joyful
scene there than when some editor appears at the bar for
public rebuke. If members of parliament had their way, press,
radio, and television would not exist, or at any rate would be
silent on political questions. Press support for a politician is
the kiss of death, though of course most members canvass for
it behind the scenes. Lloyd George obviously preferred
press lords to politicians—preferred them not only as
companions, but as ministers. He treated the House with
increasing casualness. His war cabinet was composed virtually without regard to parliamentary need; one member of
it, Smuts, served for eighteen months without ever having
any connexion with either House—a unique case; the first
full statement of war aims was made to a trade-union conference, not to the house of commons. Lloyd George often
trembled for his position. He was really in no danger so long
as he had 'the people' on his side. Every stroke which he
delivered against established authority—against admirals,
field-marshals, and conventional politicians—strengthened
him, though he often hesitated before delivering it.

The fatal mine against Lloyd George exploded almost
unnoticed, particularly by Lloyd George himself. This was
his breach with Arthur Henderson. Lloyd George had been
quicker than any other politician to grasp the importance of
the Labour movement; but he only grasped the half of it.
He regarded it as an interest just like the Free Church interest
which had originally raised him up—a pressure-group with
limited sectional objectives. He never understood the political
side of the movement. Keir Hardie seemed to him a fine
Radical pro-Boer; Ramsay MacDonald a somewhat wordy
Fabian who would one day become a Liberal minister. It is
fair to say that most Labour leaders also did not understand
the political importance of their movement until it happened.
Keir Hardie hawked the Labour leadership around to Morley,

Dilke, and Lloyd George himself; MacDonald was not indifferent to Liberal offers. Nevertheless, the Labour movement made no sense without its political content. Lloyd George never appreciated that the Labour leaders whom he praised, condescendingly, as simple working-men of sterling character were also long-standing members of the I.L.P. or the S.D.F., though not all of them remained faithful to their origin. When Lloyd George put Henderson in the war cabinet, he supposed that he was enlisting a useful agent for managing the trade unions, and Henderson modestly accepted this slighting estimate.

Nevertheless, Henderson had a special position. Lloyd George's government was composed otherwise of individuals, except for Bonar Law—men who had to depend on their personal weight and achievement. Henderson was the voice of Labour and therefore, when conflict arose, acted with an independence such as none other of Lloyd George's ministers dared to show. The question at issue was whether British Labour should attend the conference at Stockholm, to discuss possible peace terms with other Socialist parties. Henderson answered this question according to his own judgement and the outlook of the Labour party, not according to the decisions of the war cabinet. He was kept on the mat; driven to resign. Lloyd George attached little importance to the incident. He put another Labour man, George Barnes, into the war cabinet and thought that by doing so he had automatically made Barnes Labour leader, much as the king automatically made a politician leader of his party by appointing him prime minister. Nothing of the kind. Labour did not take its leader by nomination from Lloyd George, and Barnes was civilly dead so far as Labour was concerned from the moment that he entered the war cabinet. Labour continued to support the war; Labour ministers, other than Henderson, remained in office. This no doubt gave Lloyd George the illusion that nothing important had happened. He was wrong. August 1917 marked the real parting of the ways between Lloyd George and 'the people'. Labour then gave notice to quit; a notice, like so many others, deferred for the duration.

Lloyd George was secure while the war lasted. He supposed that he was even more secure when the war ended. He had fulfilled his bargain: he had won the war. The general election of December 1918 turned on the simple question whether Lloyd George should go on as prime minister. No issues of policy were at stake, despite later beliefs to the contrary. The election was a plebiscite which Lloyd George won. The Unionist and Liberal parties as such had no significance. Most electors merely wanted Lloyd George as prime minister; and, though they could express this wish only by voting for candidates who accepted the 'coupon', this was a vote against party, not a vote for Coalition Unionists or Liberals. Yet this moment of triumph saw also the appearance of a decisive threat against Lloyd George's position. He aimed, whether consciously or not, at becoming sole voice of the people by destroying the existing parties and reducing politics to a collection of individuals. The Labour party provided a new representation of the people and, as well, resurrected the two-party system just when Lloyd George had got rid of it. This was Arthur Henderson's delayed revenge for his humiliation the year before—not that so nice a man ever thought in terms of revenge. Lloyd George's Coalition was reduced from all the nation to two-thirds (a third being a generous estimate for the Liberal party). There was never at any time a hope that he could pull Labour back. Thanks to Henderson it had become fully independent: independent in its programme; independent in its constituency organizations; independent in its finance, which came from the political levy of the trade unions and not, as with the other parties, from the sale of honours.

Lloyd George was not alone in failing to read the writing on the wall. Hardly anyone did so. The defeated Asquithians thought that they would soon be back in first place on the front Opposition Bench. They were still strong in privy councillors, though weak in voters. The parliamentary Labour party was unimpressive. Its real leaders lost their seats at the general election, and it was difficult to grasp that a party of the people could be led almost as well from outside

the house as from within it, though Lloyd George himself
had played country against parliament. Henderson, with his
usual abnegation, found the predestined leader of the Labour
party in Ramsay MacDonald. He, not Lloyd George, became
the symbol, adequate or not, for the triumph of democracy.
It is fascinating to watch how Lloyd George missed the
meaning of all this. He actually wanted to see 200 Labour
members of parliament so that he could balance more adroitly
between the contending 'interests'. But where was the base
from which he could operate? During the war the 'interests'
could sink their differences in a common will to win; after the
war this uniting principle disappeared. Lloyd George made
repeated attempts to found a Centre party. This was possible only if it included representatives from both extremes.
There would be none from Labour. Therefore the Centre
party could only be another name for the Conservatives, and
they preferred their own. Even the Coalition Liberals recognized this and refused to be swallowed up, clinging to the rags
of their Radical origin—Free Trade and the Free Churches.
Lloyd George's Centre party remained a one-man band.

Lloyd George had still one asset, achievement, and he
worked it to the full. His balance sheet of success after the war
was remarkable, perhaps more so than during the war itself.
It is possible to debate how much he contributed to victory.
Lloyd George himself said that the war was won not by him,
but 'by the man in the steel helmet'. What he did after the war
was all his own doing. Peace with Germany. Lloyd George
alone, against Clemenceau and Wilson, secured a moderate
territorial settlement, which did not deprive Germany of
any 'ethnic' territory; he alone arranged reparations in such
a way that they could be settled in agreement with Germany
as soon as the Germans wanted to agree at all. Peace with
Soviet Russia. Lloyd George secured this not only against
his French allies, but against the majority of his own cabinet
including particularly Churchill. Peace with the trade unions.
Lloyd George circumvented the challenges from the railway-
men and the miners until they ceased to be dangerous. Peace
with Ireland. Lloyd George performed the miracle which had

defied every British statesman for over a century, or perhaps for five centuries—the younger Pitt, Gladstone, Asquith, to go no further back; he settled the Irish question for good and all. There was hardly a problem where he did not leave success behind him. The inter-war years lived on his legacy, and exhausted it.

Yet it was all dust and ashes. Each success lowered his reputation instead of adding to it. What went wrong? What turned Lloyd George from the most admired into the most hated and distrusted figure in British politics? It was partly his method. He defined this method in classic words: 'I was never in favour of costly frontal attacks, either in politics or war, if there were a way round.' He was the leader of a predominantly Right-wing coalition; yet his instincts were all to the Left. He did not browbeat his followers. Instead he led them with much blowing of trumpets in one direction until the moment when they discovered that he had brought them to an exactly opposite conclusion. Conciliation of Germany was prepared under a smoke-screen of 'Hang the Kaiser' and 'Make Germany Pay'. The Soviet leaders were Bolshevik untouchables until the day when Lloyd George signed a trade agreement with them. The trade-union leaders were a challenge to civilization at one moment and were being offered whisky and cigars at the next. Ireland was the supreme example. Lloyd George's successful peace was preceded by the Black and Tans, one of the most atrocious episodes in British history. The Unionists were told that Lloyd George had murder by the throat and then found themselves called upon to surrender everything which they had defended for nearly forty years. Men do not like being cheated even for the most admirable cause.

Success ruined Lloyd George in another way. Confident in his own powers, he would tolerate no rival near the throne. During the war he had colleagues of equal, or almost equal, stature—Bonar Law, Milner, Balfour. He had formidable antagonists—admirals and field-marshals. He was the little man asserting the cause of the people against great odds. After the war he reigned supreme. He had no colleagues, only subordinates; men who, however distinguished, had pinned their fate to his, and had no resources with which to oppose him. He established with them 'the relation of master and servant', which Churchill acknowledged even years later, when chancellor of the exchequer and Lloyd George a mere private member. Though Lloyd George reluctantly restored the full cabinet in place of the small war cabinet, he then disregarded it and settled policy on his own behind the scenes.

There was another terrible flaw in his position: the sale of honours. Lloyd George could plead that governments had notoriously been selling honours for the last forty years and, less directly, long before. He ran the system too hard. Not only did he sell more honours with less excuse. Lacking a party, he sold them for his own account, as the existence of the Lloyd George fund still testifies. It was one thing for him to maintain a personal dictatorship, based only on his individual gifts. The Lloyd George fund raised the threat that he would turn his disregard of party into a permanent system. Moreover, politics had to become more respectable with the advance of democracy. Corruption was an accepted necessity in the old days of a closed political nation. Appearances had to be kept up now that 'the people' had a voice in government. The integrity of Labour finance was itself a standing reproach to the older parties. Most of all, the supply of buyers was running out. It was easy to be delicate about the sale of honours when few wanted to buy them. Those who had bought honours in the past wished to elevate their position by ensuring that no one did it again, and those who still aspired to honours wished to avoid paying for them.

Some of the forces which had brought Lloyd George to power moved away from him; others lost their strength. Independent Labour removed one prop. The retreat of the businessmen from public life removed another. Some of Lloyd George's business ministers, among them the most successful, returned to their firms when the war was over; others were itching to go. Besides, Lloyd George had one great failure to set against his many successes: he could not stave off the decline of the old Liberal staples which had long been threatening. He came to power on a wave of industrial expansion which drowned financial scruples. After the war, 'the penguins of the City' enforced deflation and unemployment. The self-made businessmen who had prospered along with Lloyd George were now ruined. The Coalition Liberals vanished as abruptly as they had appeared. At the end Lloyd George was forced back on his origins. In 1922 he was hastily mobilizing the Free Churches as his last line of defence. They were no longer a decisive element in British politics, now that education had ceased to be a sectarian question. He who had once seemed the man of the future was by 1922 curiously oldfashioned. He looked, and spoke, like a Victorian. His public speeches, though still effective, sounded like echoes from the past. His audiences often took his point before he made it. His support in the press also dwindled. The press lords moved from him. He quarrelled with Northcliffe in 1918; with Riddell in 1922. Beaverbrook backed away when Bonar Law left the government. There remained only his private organ, the *Daily Chronicle*.

The fall of Lloyd George was provoked by his attempt to resist the Turkish advance on Constantinople—an attempt incidentally which, like most of his enterprises, was largely successful. This was the occasion, not the cause. He was brought down, as he had been raised up, by a revolt of the backbenchers. The Conservative meeting which ended the Coalition was actually summoned by the leaders in order to break this incipient revolt, and the rebels thought, until the last minute, that they would be defeated. It is curious how Lloyd George repeated, in every detail, the mistakes which had destroyed Asquith. He, too, came to believe that he was 'the indispensable man', safe from all storms. He, too, came to count solely on 'the talents' at the top, and disregarded the other ranks of politics—the very men in the trenches who had made him prime minister.

There was an odd outcome. The revolt of the backbenchers in 1916, which raised Lloyd George to power, destroyed the party system; their revolt of 1922, which flung him out, restored it. The rebels of 1922 acted in the name of Conservative independence. But essentially what drove them to act in this way was Labour's independence, asserted in 1918. Once Labour became a distinct party, it could be answered only by another party, not by an individual however brilliant. Lloyd George's fall dates back to the day when he kept Arthur Henderson waiting on the mat. The rise of the Labour party, which seemed to disrupt the pattern of politics, paradoxically restored the two-party system in a new form. Class became the determining factor in party allegiance, and there was no place for Lloyd George, the man who bounced from one class to another.

Lloyd George had triumphed when men wanted a national leader, who would save the country by opportunist means without regard for party principles or party ties. It is not surprising that Lenin admired him and dedicated a book to him; for Lenin, too, became great as the opportunist saviour of his country, jettisoning party doctrines of a far more rigid kind—and jettisoning party comrades also. Crisis had been Lloyd George's opportunity. Men disliked the atmosphere of crisis after the turmoil of the Great war. Even when there was a crisis, as with the general strike, the strikers solemnly played football against the police to demonstrate that nothing unusual was happening. Lloyd George had one more chance. In 1931 a financial crisis threatened, real and inescapable—or so men thought then; nowadays a chancellor of the exchequer who was faced only with the deficit of 1931 would think he was in luck's way. Ramsay MacDonald, himself at sea, invited Lloyd George to join the Labour government as leader of the House and in control of the treasury. The cuckoo seemed once more on the point of entering the nest. Lloyd George could be again the saviour of his country, inaugurating a British New Deal. At the decisive moment he was temporarily knocked out of public life by a serious operation. MacDonald and Baldwin, the two men who had destroyed him, were left to face the financial crisis as best they could. Lloyd George remained a lone voice, with no political supporters except members of his family, pathetically trying to revive the Free Church interest at great cost to his private fund. By the time of the second World war Lloyd George was too old and perhaps too jealous of others. He cast himself, if at all, in the part of a British Pétain. The former Radical was now the lamenter of past days, resentful that the great National government was composed on the basis of parties, instead of disregarding them. This final protest came appropriately from him. Lloyd George's success marked the last triumph of individual enterprise. His fall showed that the days of individual enterprise were over. Combines ruled, in politics as in everything else. Nowadays even historians work in teams.

X

THE CHIEF

ON 15 July 1921 Lord Northcliffe inspected the editorial staffs at Carmelite House. He snapped at a sub-editor: 'what was the best story in this morning's *Daily Mail*?' The sub-editor quoted: 'Viscount Northcliffe is leaving tomorrow on a world tour and will be away from England for several months.' There was a shocked silence. Northcliffe looked stern. Then he turned to his secretary: 'See that man gets a hundred-pound bonus.' Nearly everything about Northcliffe can be deduced from this story. There is the boundless arrogance, tied up with the zest for news; the nature which swung from bullying to generosity. But look a little closer. Whose leg was being pulled in the last resort—Northcliffe's or the sub's? Perhaps even ours? Many writers have had a shot at Northcliffe. They have depicted him as everything from the supreme newspaper-genius to the corrupter of English journalism. His career has been explained over and over again in terms of power. Power over the public through his newspapers; power over that great symbol of respectability, *The Times*; power in the straight political sense—either as a maker of governments or aspiring to be prime minister himself. Reading his earlier biographers, following the narrative in the *History of The Times*, accepting the trenchant sentences of Lord Beaverbrook, it was difficult to resist the impression that he was an early sketch for Adolf Hitler.

What contemporaries think of a man is, of course, highly relevant in judging him; but it is also useful to know what he thought of himself. In the biography by Reginald Pound and Geoffrey Harmsworth,[1] Northcliffe is displayed from within

[1] Reginald Pound and Geoffrey Harmsworth, *Northcliffe*.

for the first time. The result comes near to an autobiography, composed by snipping out innumerable sentences from his letters and piecing them together. This is a crushing book, with a powerful impact appropriate to its subject. It is heavy to hold, and there are nearly 900 pages to read. The reader can get through it with enjoyment only if he shares North-cliffe's own assumption that every scrap of information about himself is of intense importance, and the assumption must extend to the entire Harmsworth family. H. G. Wells, who originally suggested the book, wanted to have it called *The Harmsworth Adventure.* It would have been even more appropriate to call it *The Harmsworth Saga.* The narrative runs with the elaboration and distractions of an ancient legend. It seems incredible that many of the things in it really happened, and within recent memory. Not that the book contains anything sensational. On the contrary it knocks on the head many previous revelations confidently made or casually implied. For instance, it challenges convincingly the statement in the *History of The Times* that Northcliffe bought his peerage. All probability is the other way: Balfour, the prime minister, wished to reward Northcliffe for his assistance to Conservative newspapers in the provinces.

All the same, the book establishes one major fact about Northcliffe, the decisive fact in his life. It is not new. Others have seen it, but could not bring themselves to believe that it was the only fact about Northcliffe which counted. Hence they had to call in power or money or even wickedness as the explanation of his career. The plain fact is that Northcliffe was a newsman first, last, and all the time. He loved news and information. He loved making newspapers succeed, and he made them succeed by making them better newspapers, more crammed with information easily absorbed than any newspapers had been before. Success brought him money, and this he enjoyed spending on himself and, with erratic generosity, on others. It also brought him power—both of a political and non-political kind. This too he used, though he enjoyed it less. He tried to make English people eat standard bread, and wear the *Daily Mail* hat. He promoted flights across the

Channel and across the Atlantic. He advocated policies of a simple patriotic kind. But essentially this wielding of power was a nuisance to him, a distraction from the real business of getting out tomorrow's paper.

Take, for instance, the story of Northcliffe's relations with *The Times*. We have all been fascinated by the narrative presented in the *History of The Times*: how Northcliffe bought control and how he then set out to destroy every barrier against his autocratic will. First the 'Old Gang' had to go; then Dawson was driven out; finally Steed was sacked, and Northcliffe meant to run the paper himself as Editor-Proprietor. It is all very dramatic, and quite wrong. Naturally members of *The Times* staff think it the most important paper in the world. Northcliffe did not: he always rated the *Daily Mail* as more important and a better paper, which it was. He did not want power over *The Times*. In his boyish sentimental way, he regarded *The Times* as a national institution, and he wanted to save it, much as he contributed lavishly to the restoration of Westminster Abbey. He did not fight with the 'Old Gang' over power. He fought with them, and got them out, because they were incapable of producing an efficient newspaper. He quarrelled with Dawson over policy. He believed that Dawson was too much in the pocket of the prime minister and that he was pro-German. 'I liked Dawson very much. I had nothing against him except that he is just naturally pro-German. He can't help it.' Later events confirmed Northcliffe's opinion. As to Steed, though he was a forceful writer and a brilliant correspondent, he was not a good editor. He committed dangerous indiscretions, one of which (his rash talk in New York) brought undeserved discredit on Northcliffe. Maybe Northcliffe would have done better not to touch *The Times*. But what he did, as the *History* admits, was to put the paper on its feet financially and journalistically. This cost him much money and more worry; it brought him no advantage.

There is also an instructive story here in regard to Northcliffe's political activities. It has to do with the fall of the Asquith coalition in December 1916. On Sunday, 3 December,

Asquith and Lloyd George reached an acceptable compromise —Lloyd George to head the war committee, Asquith to remain as nominal prime minister. On Monday, 4 December, *The Times* came out with a fierce leader against Asquith. He used this as an excuse to break with Lloyd George; dissolved his government; and provoked a fight which he lost. Asquith alleged that Lloyd George had inspired *The Times* leader. Lloyd George denied it. It is now known that Dawson wrote the leader quite independently after a visit to Cliveden— inspired perhaps by Carson, certainly not by Lloyd George. But Northcliffe had seen Lloyd George on 3 December. Surely they must have conspired against Asquith? Both men denied it; they even hinted that they had not actually conversed. What was their guilty secret? It is now out and is funny, though not at all guilty. Lloyd George was insuring against failure. Being a poor man, he wanted a contract to write political articles for the *Daily Mail* and American papers. Northcliffe negotiated the contract. By 6 December Lloyd George was prime minister. Naturally he did not wish to confess that he had envisaged failure, still less that he had proposed to write for the *Daily Mail*. Nor did Northcliffe wish to confess that he had missed a catch. Hence on 8 December, 'Lord Northcliffe sees no advantage in any interview between him and the Prime Minister at this juncture.'

Of course Northcliffe had political views and expressed them strongly. He threw all his weight into winning the war just as he did into making the *Daily Mail* a success. He did his best to drive Kitchener from the war office over the shell shortage, even though he had backed the appointment in the first place. He made a tremendous contribution to Anglo-American friendship by his visit to the United States in 1917. He probably helped to destroy Austria-Hungary by his conduct of enemy propaganda. Those who denounced Northcliffe's political line really disliked his attitude towards Germany. It all depends on the point of view. The reporting of Germany in the *Daily Mail* before 1914 was, in fact, more accurate than that in the highminded Liberal press. For that matter, his insistence on reparations, however mistaken economically, was more straightforward than that of the politicians who had preached hatred of Germany and were now buttering her up for use against Russia. 'They will beat you yet, those Junkers' disturbed tender consciences. It proved to be true.

The real dislike of Northcliffe did not spring from politics. It sprang from resentment against his journalistic success. He was accused of playing down to popular taste, of giving people what they wanted. This was untrue. He set his face sternly against vulgarity or sensationalism. He did not allow 'rupture' or 'constipation' in an advertisement. He complained: ' *Merry and Bright*, No. 3. The front page is occupied by a fat man and an over-developed young woman . . . On page 6 there is a man holding a revolver.' What Northcliffe did was to give people papers which they were eager to buy, better papers in every class than those offered before. His technical innovations were two. First, he exploited the paragraph—the short, quickfire presentation which makes modern newspapers readable, the greatest advance in communication since the abandonment of Latin for English. Second, he provided accurate information of every kind. He himself read every number of each of his papers. He spotted mistakes in the advertising columns—a WANTED appearing under FOR SALE. He told his reporters to find out whether the queues outside Maypole Dairy shops were a 'crude form of advertising'. Either he was reading newsprint or asking questions. No wonder that he had little aptitude for private life. For good or ill, he remained a zestful, overgrown schoolboy, his exaggerated affection for 'the Mother' now as embarrassing as Peter Pan. He liked to be called The Chief; and *Chief* appeared invariably as the signature of his letters. This is supposed to be an importation of 'chief editor' from the United States. Was there not in it also a touch of Red Indian glamour? Northcliffe liked war-paint and bloodcurdling howls. But he also made English newspapers the best in the world; and he established the freedom of the press on the only firm foundation—the great principle that freedom must be paid for like everything else and that newspapers have a right to exist only if they can meet their bills.

PART II

XI

CROMWELL AND THE HISTORIANS

OLIVER CROMWELL, the Lord Protector, died on 3 September 1658, a figure of stormy dispute for his contemporaries and for posterity. He rose higher than any other Englishman not of royal birth; rose indeed higher than a king, for he was king and chief minister in one—the only dictator in our history. He was buried in Westminster Abbey with sovereign honours. Little more than two years later his dead body was dug up and hanged at Tyburn. The head was struck off and set on Westminster Hill; the corpse was flung into a pit beneath what is now Connaught Square.

For almost two centuries the verdict of historians went unanimously against him: knave, hypocrite, fanatic; at best, in Clarendon's phrase, 'a brave, bad man'. Then Carlyle came to his rescue: 'not a man of falsehoods, but a man of truths'. Cromwell's speeches, with their turgid, groping sincerity, spoke to the Victorian spirit. In the later nineteenth century Nonconformity, rising again in the social and political scale, took Cromwell as its first hero, and even transformed him into the founder of the Liberal party. In 1899 the man who knocked over parliaments faster than any Stuart had his statue set up at Westminster as the guardian of constitutional liberties.

The twentieth century has brought fresh praise—and new condemnation. Some Radicals have continued to admire Cromwell. After all, he cut off a king's head. Others, fortified by the evidence from the Clarke Papers, have echoed the Levellers and denounced him as the defender of oligarchy and

157

social privilege. The Puritan revolution has been given a Marxist interpretation; and Cromwell has become the champion of capitalism against a feudal monarchy—an interpretation which would have surprised him. More recently, Professor Trevor-Roper has stood Marxism on its head and presented Cromwell as the spokesman of the declining gentry who, far from being revolutionary, resented the modernity of the Court and wished to restore the good old days of Queen Elizabeth. For some, Cromwell has been the founder of the British Empire; for others, the forerunner of Robespierre and Lenin.

In fact, Cromwell was Cromwell and no one else, a puzzled country gentleman of Puritan religion with no originality of view in either politics or economics, but courageous, sincere, and above all resolute. Where others doubted and reasoned, he acted. He gave the best explanation of his career in a phrase now unbearably hackneyed but inescapable: 'No man rises so high as he who knows not whither he goes.' He had no defined policy at the beginning of the civil wars, and certainly no vision of his ultimate attainment. He knew only that the king had to be beaten in the field.

Though he never saw a battle until he was over forty, he became the best military leader in England, perhaps the best in Europe. Like Gustavus Adolphus, whom he much admired, he realized that the object of war was to win decisive battles, not to conduct manœuvres. His strategy was Napoleonic in its daring. Time and again, but particularly in the campaign that ended at Worcester, he tempted the enemy into invasion so as to destroy him the more finally. Like Napoleon, and with more justification, he won the trust and affection of his men. A great cheer went up from the whole army when, before Naseby, 'Old Ironside' rode into the camp. He repaid this affection with an equal devotion, and the reluctance of the army twice prevented him from accepting the Crown.

Politically indeed he was conservative and unconstructive. Though he resisted the tyranny of the king, he disliked almost as much the dictatorship of the rump. The theories of the Levellers were abhorrent to him. 'A nobility, a gentry, and a yeomanry—that is a good estate.' He wanted to restore the old constitution as he supposed it had existed in the time of the Tudors—crown and parliament bound together by mutual trust. It was lack of this trust which caused the civil wars and brought Charles I to the scaffold. Cromwell stepped into the vacant place and hoped by goodwill on his side to provoke goodwill in others—a hope never fulfilled. He was conservative, too, in foreign policy, dreaming of a great Protestant alliance that was long outmoded. In finance he was most conservative of all and stumbled from one expedient to the next like any Stuart.

Yet with all this he was a revolutionary too—a revolutionary in religion. He was the greatest of Independents, seeking the inner light not only for himself but respecting it in others. He 'did endeavour to discharge the duty of an honest man to God and His people's interest'. He was the first English ruler to make religious toleration the basis of his policy, even though this toleration reached its limits with Prelacy and Popery, and it is thanks to Cromwell that Dissent became a permanent element in English life. But this devotion to religion had its dangers. Cromwell sought always for God's providence, and he was only too ready to see God's hand in the victories of his own sword and the workings of his own will. God was for Cromwell what the general will was for Robespierre or the proletariat for Lenin: the justification for anything he wished to do.

Impatient in temper, choleric in disposition, he reined in his nature and strove for compromise. He had a noble record as ruler of England. No man has been a more reluctant dictator. Though power corrupted him—as it corrupts all men who touch it—there was a redeeming quality in him to the end. But in this record there stands one great blot. In the long story of crime and wickedness which comprises English rule in Ireland Cromwell has the blackest name. Ingenious apologists may excuse the massacres of Drogheda and Wexford as in accordance with the laws of war. They may even find explanations for the clearances and the transportations.

But these acts were beyond all excuse or explanation. Cromwell regarded the Irish as wild beasts who should be hunted down and exterminated, and even Englishmen who opposed him followed him in this. The Curse of Cromwell will be remembered when all else he did has been forgotten.

XII

CHARLES JAMES FOX

On 13 September 1806 Charles James Fox died in the Palladian villa of the Duke of Devonshire at Chiswick. His last words echoed the royal ancestor whom he rivalled in charm: 'It don't signify, my dearest, dearest Liz.' Charles Fox was a legend even in his lifetime. No public man has ever been so loved by his associates. He was the first statesman, incidentally, to be universally addressed by his Christian name. His picture in the National Portrait Gallery conveys something of his unique fascination—a flushed stout man, sitting on a stile in disarray amid the delights of Nature: a welcome contrast indeed to the formal figures who surround him on the walls. Many historians have seen in Fox a charmer and nothing more; a blundering tactician greedy for power; an irresponsible declaimer who drove himself and his followers from one disaster to another.

The picture has a touch of truth. Fox had an incurable love for members of the great Whig families. There was something absurd in a champion of the people who set up a ministry composed predominantly of dukes and marquises. His private life did not show that austere morality which the British public expects from its leaders. Other Whigs, including his father, made fortunes from the service of the state; Charles Fox lost an even vaster fortune on the race-course and at the gambling tables. His father, Lord Holland, brought him up on the doctrine: 'The young are always right; the old are always wrong.' Everyone knows the story of Lord Holland's remark when Charles smashed a gold watch: 'If you must, you must.' On the same principle Lord Holland provided £300,000 to

161

F

pay his son's more pressing debts. Charles himself tried to meet this same need by running a faro-bank at Brooks's—a bank which he continued to run even when he was secretary of state for foreign affairs.

When all else had failed, his aristocratic friends had a whip round and provided him with £3,000 a year. 'How will he take it?' one of them asked anxiously. Another gave the correct reply: 'Quarterly, I suppose.' Gambling, drinking and late hours did not exhaust his vices. He had a number of natural children, all of whom he adored. He lived with Mrs. Armitstead, 'dearest Liz', for nearly twenty years before he married her—she had grown rich by living previously with other men. Then he kept his marriage secret so that he might continue to flaunt the immorality which he was no longer practising. If there was only his love of Nature and the classics to set off against all this, we should say that he was a curious character, an amusing period piece, no more; certainly not worth commemoration.

But there is a great deal more. For one thing, Fox invented the modern British constitution—invented, that is, the two-party system and the doctrine that the crown must accept as prime minister the political leader favoured by a majority of the house of commons. Earlier politicians had in fact 'opposed'; but they wrapped up their opposition as patriotic advice or took shelter under the patronage of the heir-apparent. Fox criticized whatever was done by the government of the day and claimed on every issue that he could have done better; he was the first leader of a formed and avowed Opposition. Again, earlier politicians had forced their unwelcome services on the King, but always with loyal apologies and in the belief that the favour of the crown would bring with it support from the house of commons, not the other way round. Fox, with a gambler's extremism, resolved to win or lose all; he regarded George III as Satan and held that the crown should be reduced to a cipher. 'The Crown is endowed with no faculty whatever of a private nature.'

Charles Fox lost in his lifetime, but he won the future. In the words of Richard Pares: 'George III undoubtedly beat

Charles Fox in 1784, and trampled on his ghost in 1807; but our politicians act, today, on Charles Fox's constitutional principles.' It was evidence of Fox's triumph when Victoria had to accept Gladstone as prime minister in spite of her violent protest, and even more striking evidence when George V sent for Ramsay MacDonald in 1924 with no protest at all. We are supposed to owe the British constitution to the wisdom of our ancestors. It would be truer to say that in its present form it sprang fully grown from Charles Fox's personal hostility to George III. The 'Whig interpretation of history' is a horse from the same stable. Fox asserted, quite wrongly, that his view of the constitution had flourished ever since the Glorious Revolution. His Whig friends echoed this belief, and historians followed suit until they were put right in our own day by Sir Lewis Namier.

This political doctrine makes Fox interesting, important, even great; it does not make him admirable. What gave him a unique place in English history was his championing of liberty, both individual and national. He was a long time coming to it. In his early days he had a wrongheaded enthusiasm for the house of commons—even defending its right to expel and disqualify Wilkes. The revolt of the American colonies taught him that there were more important things than legal niceties or the struggle for political power. Fox was among the first to advocate the complete independence of America, and he staked his political career on this cause until it was won. The impeachment of Warren Hastings, which he shared with Burke, took him a stage farther. However doubtful the detailed charges, that case established the principle that the British Empire was something more than an empire of exploitation.

Fox's finest hour came with the war against the French Revolution. All calculation of personal advantage was swept aside. Fox could have been a leading war minister. He, not Pitt, would have been 'the pilot who weathered the storm'. Fox never considered this course for a moment. He was convinced that the war was unnecessary and morally wrong. Almost alone among Englishmen of the governing class, he recognized the principle of liberty in France in spite of the violence of the Terror, and he was convinced that Great Britain was fighting on the side of tyranny. He broke with his closest friends and for five years argued against the war almost single-handed. There is no more glorious story in our history. Sixty years later Richard Cobden, contemplating a similar course of action himself, wrote of Fox:

It is impossible to read the speeches of Fox at this time without feeling one's heart yearn with admiration and gratitude for the bold and resolute manner in which he opposed the war, never yielding and never repining, under the most discouraging defeats. The annals of Parliament do not record a nobler struggle in a nobler cause.

Here again Fox lost the present and won the future. He saw his supporters in the house shrink from fifty to twenty; he was struck off the privy council for toasting 'Our Sovereign Lord, the People'; police spies were set on him, and Pitt considered sending him to the Tower. But posterity has confirmed his judgement on this war for despotism, and in the nineteenth century British policy welcomed the liberal revolutions which Pitt had tried to suppress. The spirit of Fox prevails whenever England stands on the side of Freedom. The independence of Ireland and India are his memorials, and those who now champion the peoples of Africa are only the latest who belong to 'the party of Mr. Fox'.

XIII

METTERNICH AND HIS 'SYSTEM'

In 1822, just before the opening of the congress of Verona, the Russian ambassador suddenly died. Metternich is supposed to have said: 'I wonder why he did that.' An old story, probably made up years later as a parody of Metternich's habit of finding a hidden significance in every event. At any rate there is no need to search for the significance in Metternich's own death on 11 June 1859. The significance hits one in the eye. The battle of Solferino was fought a fortnight later. The Austrian army was defeated by the combined forces of France and Sardinia. Austrian supremacy in Italy was ended, and the age of Metternich ended with it.

Solferino was not much of a battle except for the terrible casualties. It was a brutal slogging match. Neither side showed any gift of leadership or strategical insight. All the same, it was a decisive battle; the first lasting success of European nationalism. National Italy and, more remotely, national Germany were born on the field of Solferino. More distantly still, all the national states of east-central Europe can trace their victory back to the same day. The illdirected armies, lurching clumsily against each other, symbolized the clash of two great principles: the conservative tradition of dynastic rights on the one side, revolutionary nationalism on the other. No wonder that Metternich withdrew from the scene. He and his Europe died together.

As a matter of fact, Metternich dated his own death rather earlier. 'Yes, we are all dead', he said to his wife on 13 March 1848, when he came home after resigning as Austrian chancellor under the pressure of street rioting. The revolutions of 1848 were all directed against 'the Metternich system'—against the social system which he was supposed to represent; against the international settlement made at the Congress of Vienna; and against the conservative principles which Metternich enunciated at such length. In March 1848 he supposed that the revolution had triumphed. He went into exile—at Brighton oddly enough, though that is symbolic, too. In fact the revolutions were defeated. The old order had another ten years of existence, though hardly of life. Metternich himself got back to Vienna: a neglected ghost to whom nobody listened.

The Italian war of 1859 saw the next round in the struggle and a more decisive one. This time the national cause triumphed for good. But in a different way from 1848. Then men had believed that the idealist cause would triumph of its own weight. 'Italy will do it herself.' And not only Italy—Poland, Germany, Hungary, radicalism, democracy, socialism: they were all supposed to be irresistible; and they were all defeated. Solferino was not a bit like that. It was won by conventional, disciplined armies in an oldfashioned way, and the war was brought about by old-style secret diplomacy— the successors of Metternich were outwitted by his own methods. Though conservatism was defeated at Solferino, radicalism was defeated too. This set the pattern for the future. All the great radical hopes of 1848 were achieved within a couple of generations. But they were achieved in a hardheaded cynical way, and by the time they arrived they had lost their glamour. Though there were celebrations of a rather modest sort on the field of Solferino in 1959, no one said, as Charles Fox said of the fall of the Bastille: 'How much the greatest event since the beginning of the world—and how much the best.'

Metternich's system has gone. There are national states all over Europe. Men contemplate this outcome gloomily. They even regret that they did not take Metternich's advice and leave things alone. Indeed it is the fashion now among historians to go wandering about the past regretting what has happened. I do not share this contemporary taste. It is equally little the task of the historian to be for ever rejoicing in what happened, or to keep pointing out—as Macaulay did —that events were on the move, faster and faster, to that most perfect of times: the present. The great thing about the past is that it has happened—very fortunately for historians. It is hard enough to find out about it without trying to alter it. Least of all can we put it back. So-called restorations simply create new systems and institutions with the old names. This is how it worked out with the great Restoration which followed the defeat of Napoleon. Even the Austrian empire of 1815 was markedly different—in structure, spirit, geographic shape—from the anonymous empire which had stumbled into war with the French revolution in 1792. It was this remade empire that Metternich spent his life defending, and which we now see through a romantic haze.

Even the haze of time is a romantic illusion. The Austrian empire is supposed to have been extremely old. Strictly speaking, it was quite new. The title, Emperor of Austria, was invented only in 1804, to have something to set off against Napoleon's own invention, Emperor of the French. As for the Austrian empire, as distinct from the emperor, I am not sure that it ever existed at all. It was an idea, not a state; or, on a more prosaic level, a convenient name for the territorial possessions, shifting and scattered, of the House of Habsburg.

Other dynasties managed to associate themselves, more or less, with some sort of national consciousness long before the age of nationalism. The House of Habsburg remained purely a family concern. It is often called 'international', but this is the wrong word. International implies cooperation between nations or at any rate between nationalities. The House of Habsburg did not want nations and nationalities to cooperate; it did not want them to exist. The Austrian empire was not international; it was 'non-national', as indeed it was nega- tive in everything. From start to finish the Habsburg monarchy could be defined only in terms of what it was not. In the sixteenth century it was not Turkish. Later on, it was not aggressive—a slightly sham claim this one. At the end, it

was not German. It had many fine mottoes and maxims. Its
real spirit was expressed by the lines of Hilaire Belloc:

> Always keep a-hold of Nurse
> For fear of finding something worse—

or, for that matter, something better.

It was this negative character that suited Metternich, and
led him to serve the House of Habsburg for a lifetime. At
least, this is the more charitable interpretation of his conduct:
the public face, as it were, with which historians credit
statesmen. As a matter of fact, he served the House of
Habsburg because he made a fortune out of it: turned from a
count into a prince, acquired castles and palaces, lined his
pockets. Certainly Metternich and the Habsburg monarchy
were well in tune. It had always been negative; he was the
great 'No-man'. One can make a long list of the changes he
did not like, from the French revolution to the change of date
on New Year's day. But what did he like except economic
amelioration for his own benefit? He claimed to like railways,
but this was only to move troops about better for purposes
of resistance. In old age he used to sit at his desk, consoling
himself with the murmur 'I have been a rock of order.'

This was largely pretence: deception of others and still
more of himself. Metternich was no rock. He was obstinate,
but soft, always trying to talk difficulties out of existence. He
made his name as the man who organized Europe for the
overthrow of Napoleon. But he had not intended to do it.
What he wanted was to turn Napoleon—the conqueror and
tyrant of Europe—into a gentle, bumbling familyman,
devoted to his silly Habsburg wife. The Habsburg monarchy
was much the same—resisting in the last ditch, not the first.
It had to save Europe from Mohammedanism in the sixteenth
century when the Turks actually reached the gates of Vienna.
But it undertook the task unwillingly; more than a century
and a half passed before it liberated Hungary; and even this
had to be provoked by another Turkish siege of Vienna.

So, too, in the nineteenth century, after the defeat of
Napoleon, Metternich deliberately did not reclaim the

Austrian Netherlands and the old Habsburg lands on the Rhine. Others could have the honour and the burden of meeting the next wave of French aggression. The Habsburg emperor refused also to restore the Holy Roman Empire in Germany, leaving the German princes to resist nationalism. On the other hand, the Habsburg monarchy, under Metternich's guidance, pushed itself into Italy more assertively than before. This is a puzzle, a contradiction. Metternich did not like trouble if it could be avoided. Yet in Italy the Habsburg monarchy acquired new territories; distributed guarantees to the princes; and deliberately marked itself out as the target for nationalism.

I doubt whether there is a rational explanation for this policy. The Italian peninsula was a power vacuum after the fall of Napoleon, and the Habsburg monarchy got sucked into it. The Great Powers have always felt the glamour of Italy, and statesmen have attached more strategic importance to it than it had in reality, from Charles VIII of France in 1494 to Winston Churchill in 1943. Metternich made the same miscalculation. Besides, he believed that Italy was more favourable ground on which to conduct the struggle against revolutionary ideas. In Germany, he had little faith in the princes; he recognized the strength of German nationalism, and felt its appeal himself. Italian nationalism was an ideal, pure abstraction. There had never been any kind of Italian national state before the time of Napoleon, and even his Kingdom of Italy was a sham. Italy was, in Metternich's well-known phrase, a geographic expression, without even a unity of language—what we nowadays call 'Italian' used to be called 'Tuscan'. The Italian states had a glorious historical record. Venice, Florence, and the Papacy were already flourishing, when most of the contemporary Great Powers had not been heard of. The conflict between tradition and abstract ideal was sharpest and clearest in Italy. It was the best field of conflict for Metternich to choose if he were determined to fight at all. Italy became the parade-ground both of his policy and of the Habsburg army.

A man who conducts the foreign policy of a great power for

almost forty years cannot concentrate all the time on a single problem; and Italian affairs were often obscured by Poland, Spain, the Eastern question, Belgium, and even at one moment by Switzerland. Nevertheless Italy always occupied the central position in Metternich's calculations. Italy was to demonstrate his own skill. It was to convince everyone that the Habsburg monarchy was 'a European necessity'. Instead it worked the other way round. It was Italy which first created the moral discredit of the Habsburg monarchy. Think of the English poets denouncing Metternich and Austria—Byron, Landor, Swinburne, the Brownings; it was experience in Italy which moved them. Think of Gladstone exclaiming: 'There is not an instance—there is not a spot upon the whole map where you can lay your finger and say, "There Austria did good!"' The spot where in fact he laid his finger was Naples—a kingdom which was kept in existence by Austrian protection.

Elsewhere in Europe others shared the blame for oppression: Russia, for instance, shared it in Poland, and indeed deserved the greater share. In Italy the Habsburg empire oppressed alone. Austrian rule in Italy appeared as one of the two big moral blots on nineteenth-century Europe— Turkish rule in the Balkans was the other. It was Italy which turned the Austrian empire into a second 'sick man'. The moral defeat went further. Even after Italy had been liberated and united, the moral smear remained; and when the nationalities of the Austrian empire voiced their claims during the first World war, they soon found sympathetic hearers. Englishmen and Americans had grown up believing that Austria once oppressed the Italians; therefore they readily believed that she was now oppressing the Czechs, Rumanians, and south Slavs. It was Austrian rule in Italy that launched her on the path of disintegration.

The Austrian defeat in Italy was a European defeat, not simply a defeat by Italian nationalism. This is what Solferino symbolizes. And this is why Italians rejoiced less over the anniversary of the success at Solferino than they did eleven years ago over the anniversary of the unsuccessful revolutions of 1848. In 1848 the Habsburg monarchy had contended against the Italian revolution without interference from foreign powers. The British government advised the Habsburgs to give up their Italian possessions—in its usual generous way with other people's property. The French republicans sympathized with Italian nationalism, but not to the extent of going to war. The Austrian army fought alone, and won alone. Afterwards things changed. Austrian rule, now based on martial law, was in fact more oppressive than it had been before. The other powers wearied of 'the Italian question'. Once they had perhaps agreed that Austrian rule in Italy was a European necessity. Now they came to feel that the European necessity was to get Austria out of Italy, and all the Great Powers welcomed Austria's defeat in 1859.

There was another factor on which Italian historians have recently laid much stress. The movements of 1848 had relied solely on the national ideal; and this appealed only to the intellectual middle class. After 1848 Mazzini went on preaching nationalism, but others thought that they must add social appeals if they were to win the masses: land reform for the peasants; social reform for the workers in the towns. There was no longer the old choice between acquiescence and revolution. The question for Italians was now: Which sort of revolution? A great radical revolution on the French scale of 1789, or a respectable revolution with moderate methods and foreign allies? Cavour, prime minister of Sardinia, chose the second course. From the moment he came to power in 1852 he regarded it as his task to expel the Austrians without shaking the social foundations. He, not Metternich—or rather Metternich's successors—was now the true conservative.

The Italian war of 1859 was made by diplomacy, not by popular enthusiasm. The revolution was there, but it came from without: Napoleon III, himself a revolutionary, turned respectable, or at any rate turned emperor. The Austrian army was defeated, not morally overwhelmed. Solferino was not the end of the story, only the beginning. Garibaldi, the great radical, won Sicily and Naples by radical methods in

1860. But Cavour was too strong for him. Garibaldi abandoned the social revolution for the sake of Italian unity. Not much more than twenty years later, Italy became the ally of the Habsburg monarchy. More ironical still, in the nineteen-thirties, after the dissolution of the Austrian empire, Dollfuss and Schuschnigg—the last Austrian statesmen who claimed to be the heirs of Metternich—were kept going by Mussolini's protection. Now, strangely enough, all the Great Powers are agreed that Austria is a European necessity. It is about the only thing on which they are agreed. And they are agreed upon it because the Austrian empire, the empire of Metternich, has ceased to exist. He is dead all right.

XIV

GENOCIDE

WHEN British forces entered the so-called 'convalescent camp' at Belsen in 1945, they found a scene of indescribable horror: the wasted bodies of 50,000 human beings who had died from starvation and disease. Kramer, 'the beast of Belsen', and his assistants were hanged for this atrocious crime. Only a century before, all Ireland was a Belsen. Nearly two million Irish people died of starvation and fever within five years; another million fled, bearing disease to Liverpool and the New World.

The story can be told in general terms, presenting the famine as a natural catastrophe like an earthquake. The population of Ireland had greatly increased in the preceding years —why, no one knows. Most of the people depended almost exclusively on the potato. In 1845 potato blight arrived, apparently from America. It was a fungus which rotted first the plants and then the potatoes in the clamps. A run of wet summers helped the spread of the blight. The potato harvest failed four years running. The Irish peasants had no reserves to fall back on. Many of their landlords were harsh; some almost as impoverished as their peasants—thought it is not recorded that any landlord died of starvation. It all happened because it had to happen.

This is how historians usually treat the past. We explain, and with that our duty is finished. The dead are dead. They have become so many figures in a notebook. But they were once human beings, and other human beings sent them to their death. The blight was 'natural'; the failure of the potato crop was 'natural'. After that, men played a part. There was food available to save the Irish people from starvation. It was denied them. Nor did Ireland stand alone. Ireland was at this time part of the United Kingdom, the wealthiest country in the world. The British government had insisted on undertaking responsibility for Ireland. When crisis arose, they ran away from it. The men in Whitehall were usually of humane disposition and the bearers of honoured names: Lord John Russell; Sir Charles Wood, later first Viscount Halifax; Sir Charles Trevelyan. These men, too, were in a sense victims. They were gripped by the most horrible, and perhaps the most universal, of human maladies: the belief that principles and doctrines are more important than lives. They imagined that rules, invented by economists, were as 'natural' as the potato blight. Trevelyan, who did most to determine events, always wanted to leave Ireland to 'the operation of natural causes'. He refused to recognize that only the gigantic operation of an artificial cause—the exertion of British power —prevented the Irish people from adopting the natural remedy, and eating the food which was available for them. Like most members of the comfortable classes at all times, he regarded the police and the law courts as natural phenomena.

Mrs. Woodham-Smith in her most admirable and thorough book[1] writes: 'The 1840s must not be judged by the standards of today.' Of course she is right, even though she goes on to judge, and to condemn, the British government. Russell, Wood and Trevelyan were highly conscientious men, and their consciences never reproached them. Nor are the standards of today much to rely on. The British rulers of the 1840s were no worse than those who later sent millions of men to their deaths in two world wars; no worse than those who now plan to blow all mankind to pieces for the sake of some principle or other. But they were also no better. Though they killed only two million Irish people, this was not for want of trying. Jowett once said:

> I have always felt a certain horror of political economists since I heard one of them say that the famine in Ireland would not kill more than a million people, and that would scarcely be enough to do much good.

[1] Cecil Woodham-Smith, *The Great Hunger*.

The successors of these economists are the same in spirit. They preach the virtue of a little healthy unemployment, and do not reply on the whip of starvation only because it has been taken from their hands. If the particular crime committed in Ireland a century ago could not happen now, it is not because present-day statesmen are an improvement on their predecessors. It is because the common conscience of mankind no longer allows statesmen to live up to their principles.

Here was the peculiar tragedy of the Irish famine. The common conscience failed to work, or at least did not work effectively. It is easy to understand how Trevelyan and the rest thought that they were doing their duty. They were handling human beings as ciphers on a bit of paper. They looked up the answers in a textbook of economics without ever once setting eyes on the living skeletons of the Irish people. They invented a distinction between those who were starving because of the potato blight and those starving from normal distress. They excused the Irish for being hit by the blight once. They condemned them for persisting in planting potatoes after blight appeared—as though the Irish could do anything else. Most of all, these enlightened men feared that the whole social structure would topple down if men and women were once given food which they could not pay for.

Not all Englishmen were enlightened in this way. This was already the England of good works, the England which emancipated the slaves and ended child labour, the England which repealed the Corn Laws and brought sanitation to the towns. The public conscience was in many ways more sensitive, quicker to respond, than it is now. It responded over Ireland, though not enough. The British government did much when it was in the hands of Sir Robert Peel. They contributed the stupendous sum of £8 million to meet the first disaster of 1845; set up relief organizations and public works on a scale never attempted before. Peel's fall from office in 1846 was an additional disaster for Ireland. He was never one to confess impotence, and he might have been

powerful enough to override even the principles of Sir
Charles Trevelyan.

Official and private individuals in Ireland did all that men
could do. Doctors died of fever. Administrators drove themselves to death, and often provided relief out of their own
pockets. Trevelyan complained that his Commissariat officers
could 'bear anything but the ceaseless misery of the children'.
The British Relief Association raised large sums, including
£2,000 from Queen Victoria. The Society of Friends had a
record of spotless honour, as often happens when men are
suffering. Quakers contributed money, ran their own system
of relief, sacrificed their lives. All these efforts touched only
the edge of the famine. Everything combined against the
Irish people. Ignorance played a large part. Even capable Irish
administrators did not grasp that there were no harbours on
the west coast which could discharge cargoes of food. No
enterprising newspaper correspondent described the horrors
in Ireland for the English press as Russell was to describe the
lesser horrors in the Crimea nine years later. Nearly all
Englishmen regarded Ireland as an inferior version of England, inhabited by lazier and less efficient people. The Irish
administrators themselves were bewildered that the problems
of Ireland could not be somehow solved by the well-tried
methods of the poor rate, boards of guardians and the workhouse test. In many districts there was no one to pay the poor
rate, or to sit on the board of guardians; most of the Irish
would have regarded an English workhouse as a haven of
luxury.

The ignorance was often wilful. Men make out that a problem does not exist when they do not know how to solve it. So
it was in all English dealings with Ireland. Again, the famine
went on so long. English people, and even the British government, were ready to do something for one hard season. They
were exasperated out of their pity when the blight reappeared
year after year. How were they to understand that the blight,
hitherto unknown, would settle permanently in the soil and
would flourish every wet summer? It was easy to slip into the
belief that the blight was the fault of the Irish themselves.

They were a feckless people; the blight was worse in Ireland than in England; the self-righteous conclusion was obvious. English antagonism was not turned only against the Irish poor. Though the landlords are often supposed to represent a common Anglo-Irish interest, Englishmen and their government were as hostile to Irish landlords as to Irish peasants. At the height of the famine the full system of the English poor law was extended to Ireland. This was quite as much to make life unpleasant for the landlords as to benefit the starving. The Irish landlords were 'very much like slave holders with white slaves . . . they had done nothing but sit down and howl for English money'. Lord John Russell doubted whether 'taken as a whole the exertions of property for the relief of distress have been what they ought to have been'. The starving tenants could not pay their rent. Yet landlords were told to relieve them out of the rents which they could not pay. Some landlords were still prosperous. A few contributed honourably. Most did their duty by keeping up a sumptuous estate, which is what landlords are for.

The Irish people were driven off their land. They were starved, degraded, treated worse than animals. They lamented, they suffered, they died. Yet they made hardly an attempt at resistance. This is perhaps the most dreadful part of the story—a people allowing themselves to be murdered. Mrs. Woodham-Smith suggests that the Irish were physically too weak to resist, that famine only gave a final push to their perpetual course of misery and want. Surely it was more than that. Centuries of English tyranny had destroyed Irish will and Irish confidence. O'Connell told the House of Commons in his last speech: 'Ireland is in your hands, in your power. If you do not save her, she cannot save herself.' The few political leaders in Ireland themselves accepted the economic doctrines of their conquerors. They demanded Repeal of the Union, not a reform of the landed system, and Repeal was the cause which brought Smith O'Brien to the widow McCormack's cabbage patch in his attempt at rebellion in 1848. This provided a farcical note at the end of the tragic story.

Yet not quite the end, which was more farcical still. The

English governing class ran true to form. They had killed two million Irish people. They abused the Irish for disliking this. Lord John Russell said in 1848:

We have subscribed, worked, visited, clothed, for the Irish, millions of money, years of debate, etc., etc., etc. The only return is rebellion and calumny.

Lastly, a gesture of forgiveness no doubt by the British government for the crimes which they had committed in Ireland, royalty was trundled out. Queen Victoria and Prince Albert visited Ireland. They were received everywhere with great enthusiasm.

The famine did not end in Ireland. It was repeated year after year, sometimes in milder form. Natural causes did their work. The Society of Friends alone saw the condition of Ireland in its true light. In 1849 they refused to act any longer as a relief agency. Only the government, they wrote, 'could carry out the measures necessary in many districts to save the lives of the people'. 'The condition of our country has not improved in spite of the great exertions made by charitable bodies.' It could not be improved until the land system of Ireland was reformed, which was a matter for legislation, not philanthropy. The British government ignored the Quakers' advice. Nothing was done for Ireland until an embittered and more resolute generation of Irishmen acted for themselves.

XV

WHO BURNT THE REICHSTAG?

ON the evening of 27 February 1933, the Reichstag building in Berlin was set on fire and went up in flames. This was a stroke of good fortune for the Nazis. Although Hitler had been appointed chancellor by President Hindenberg on 30 January, the Nazis did not have a parliamentary majority, even with their Nationalist allies. The Reichstag was dissolved, and the Nazis began a raging electoral campaign. They were still doubtful of success. They badly needed a 'Red' scare. On 24 February the police raided Communist headquarters. It was announced that they had discovered plans for a Communist revolution. Evidently they did not discover much: the alleged subversive documents were never published. Then came the burning of the Reichstag. Here was the Red scare ready-made. On the following day, Hindenburg promulgated an emergency decree 'for the protection of the People and the State'. The constitutional guarantees of individual liberty were suspended. The Nazis were able to establish a legal reign of terror. Thanks partly to this, they and the Nationalists won a bare majority at the general election on 5 March; thereafter, first the Communist party, and then all parties other than the National Socialist, were made illegal. The burning of the Reichstag helped to clear the way for Hitler's dictatorship.

Who then committed the decisive act? Who actually started the Reichstag fire? The Nazis said it was the work of Communists. They tried to establish this verdict at the trial of the supposed incendiaries before the High Court at Leipzig. They failed. Hardly anyone now believes that the

179

Communists had a hand in the Reichstag fire. If not the
Communists, then who? People outside Germany, and many
inside it, found a simple answer: the Nazis did it themselves.
This version has been generally accepted. It appears in most
textbooks. The most reputable historians, such as Alan
Bullock, repeat it. I myself accepted it unquestioningly, without looking at the evidence. A German civil servant, Fritz
Tobias, with no Nazi sympathies, recently looked at the
evidence. His results are surprising.

Shortly before nine o'clock, on the evening of 27 February,
a student of theology called Hans Flöter, now a lecturer in
Bremen, was going home after a day in the library. As he
crossed the open space in front of the Reichstag, he heard
the sound of breaking glass. He looked up, and saw someone
climbing into the Reichstag through a window on the first
floor. Otherwise, the place was deserted. Flöter ran to the
corner, found a policeman. 'Someone is breaking into the
Reichstag.' The two men ran back. Through the window they
saw not only a shadowy figure but flames. It was three
minutes past nine. Flöter had done his duty. He went home
to his supper and out of the story. Another passer-by joined
the policeman: a young printer called Thaler, who was incidentally a Social Democrat. He died in 1943. Thaler shouted
out: 'Shoot, man, shoot.' The policeman raised his revolver,
and fired. The shadowy figure disappeared. The policeman
ran back to the nearest police post, and gave the alarm. The
time was recorded as 9.15. Within minutes police poured
into the Reichstag. At 9.22, a police officer tried to enter the
debating chamber. He was driven back by the flames. At
9.27, the police discovered and arrested a half-naked young
man. He was a Dutchman called Marinus van der Lubbe.

Meanwhile, the firebrigade had also been alarmed. The
first report reached them at 9.13. The first engine reached the
Reichstag at 9.18. There were inevitable delays. Only one
side-door was kept unlocked after eight o'clock in the evening.
The firemen, who did not know this, went to the wrong door.
Then they wasted time putting out small fires in the passages.
There was confusion as one alarm crossed another. The full

strength of the Berlin firebrigade—some sixty engines—was mobilized only at 9.42. By then, the chamber was irreparably lost. It still stands, an empty shell.

There was an alarm of a different kind. Just across the road from the Reichstag was the house of its president, the Nazi leader Goering. But Goering had not moved in. The house, or Palace, was unoccupied except for a flat at the top which Goering had lent to Putzi Hanftstaengel, an upper-class hanger-on of the Nazis. Hanftstaengel looked out of his window and saw the Reichstag burning. He knew that Hitler and Goebbels were at a party near by. He telephoned Goebbels. Goebbels thought this was one of Hanftstaengel's practical jokes and put down the phone. Hanftstaengel rang again. Goebbels checked with the Reichstag and found the report was true. Within a few minutes he and Hitler and a swarm of Nazi attendants were also in the Reichstag. An English journalist, Sefton Delmer, managed to slip in with them. Hitler was beside himself with frenzy: 'This is a Communist plot, the signal for an uprising. Every Communist official must be shot. The Communist M.P.s must be hanged.' Maybe he already saw the advantages. If so, those standing by were all taken in. To them Hitler appeared as a man surprised, outraged, even fearful.

Van der Lubbe was taken to the nearest police station. He was interrogated until three in the morning. Then he slept, was given breakfast, and at 8 a.m. questioned again. He gave clear, coherent answers. He described how he had entered the Reichstag; where he had started fires, first with the aid of four fire-lighters, then by stripping off his garments and setting light to them. The police checked his story by going round the Reichstag according to his statement with a stopwatch. They found that it fitted precisely up to the moment of his arrest. Van der Lubbe was clear about his motive. He had hoped that the entire German people would protest against the Nazi government. When this did not happen, he determined that one individual at any rate should make his protest. Although the burning of the Reichstag was certainly a signal for revolt—a 'beacon' he called it—he had given the signal alone. He denied steadily that he had any associates. He knew no Nazis. He was not a Communist—that is, he was not a member of the Communist party. He was, in fact, a Socialist with vaguely left-wing views. Van der Lubbe also described his movements during the previous weeks, drifting across Germany from one casual ward to another; he even described the shops where he had bought fire-lighters and matches. Here, too, the police checked his story. Every detail was correct. The police officers concluded that he was unbalanced, but more than usually intelligent, with an exceptionally accurate sense of place and direction. His interrogators were experienced men, without political commitment. They were convinced that he was speaking the truth and that he had set fire to the Reichstag all alone. The officers of the firebrigade were also agreed that, so far as they could tell, the Reichstag had burnt exactly as van der Lubbe said it had.

This did not do for Hitler and the other Nazi leaders. They had committed themselves from the first moment to the view that the burning of the Reichstag was a Communist plot. Whether they believed this or not, it had to be sustained before the German public. When van der Lubbe came to trial, four others stood in the dock with him: Torgler, leader of the Communist group in the Reichstag, and three Bulgarian Communists who were living in Germany, one of them the famous Dimitrov. The trial before the High Court at Leipzig had little to do with van der Lubbe. He had been found in the Reichstag; he had started fires; the case against him was so clear as to be hardly worth making. The public prosecutor and the Nazi government behind him were concerned to pin the guilt on the four Communists. They failed entirely. Torgler had been in his room in the Reichstag until 8 p.m. Then he left; witnesses saw him go. All was then quiet in the Reichstag. There was no evidence to connect him with van der Lubbe. As to Dimitrov and the two other Bulgarians, there was no evidence to connect them either with van der Lubbe or with the fire. This was awkward for the High Court judges. They were conscientious lawyers, not Nazis. They would not condemn individuals without evidence.

But they were willing to please the Nazi government where no flagrant injustice to individuals seemed to be involved.

The High Court therefore listened complacently while so-called experts demonstrated that the fire could not have been started by one man on his own. Perhaps the High Court even believed the experts, as judges sometimes do. These experts were not fire officers, policemen, or fire assessors. They were professors of chemistry and criminology, who laid down theories about the fire without even visiting the Reichstag. Van der Lubbe was in despair. He had meant to shake Nazi rule. Instead, he had consolidated their dictatorship and, as well, involved innocent men. For most of the time he remained broken and detached, his head sunk on his chest. Some people attributed this to drugs. Independent psychologists who examined him thought that there was nothing wrong with him except despair. Once he came to the surface. For six hours he tried to convince the judges that he had started the fires all alone. He spoke clearly, coherently, accurately. A Dutch observer—himself an experienced criminal judge— was persuaded that van der Lubbe was speaking the truth. The German judges thought otherwise. With unshakeable prejudice, they stormed and bullied. How, they asked, could he withstand the evidence of expert witnesses? Van der Lubbe answered: 'I was there, and they were not. I know it can be done because I did it.'

The High Court arrived at a strange verdict. Van der Lubbe was found guilty, and, though arson was not a capital crime when he committed his offence, Hitler made it so by retrospective law. Van der Lubbe was duly sentenced to death and executed by beheading with an axe. The four Communists were acquitted, but the judges recorded that van der Lubbe must have had assistants. The Reichstag there-fore was burnt by persons unknown, and the Nazis had to be satisfied with the implication that these mysterious persons, never seen and vanishing without trace, were Communists. Hardly anyone now accepts this verdict. If the Nazis, with all the resources of dishonesty and of the German state, failed to produce any real evidence against the Communists, we may safely conclude that the Communists had nothing to do with the burning of the Reichstag. But nearly everyone accepts part of the High Court verdict. They agree that van der Lubbe could not have set fire to the Reichstag all on his own. And, since his associates were not Communists, who could they be? Who but those who benefited from the fire—Hitler and the Nazis themselves? Dimitrov already seized on this interpretation while the trial was proceeding. As a good Communist, he was concerned to attack the Nazis, not to save himself. Therefore he hardly bothered to demonstrate his own innocence, which was indeed obvious enough. He grasped at the evidence of the experts, endorsed it, under-lined its implications. When Goering was in the box, Dimitrov said to him more or less straight out: 'Van der Lubbe had help. He did not get it from me. Therefore he got it from you.' Goering found it difficult to beat off this charge without repudiating the expert evidence which the Nazis were putting forward. Hence his almost inarticulate rage.

Nor was this all. German Communists in exile, led by the redoubtable Willi Münzenberg, took up the Reichstag fire as a wonderful instrument for anti-Nazi propaganda. They published a Brown Book of alleged evidence about it. They staged a counter-trial in London that duly brought in a verdict of guilty against the Nazis. Münzenberg and his collaborators were a jump ahead of the Nazis. Not only had they the evidence of the experts, demonstrating that van der Lubbe could not have done it alone and therefore implicating the Nazis; they also produced a mass of evidence to show how the Nazis had done it. The vital point here was an under-ground passage from Goering's house to the Reichstag, which carried electric and telephone cables and pipes for central heating. Through this passage some S.A. men (Brown Shirts) were supposed to have entered the Reichstag. Then they either soaked the curtains and woodwork in some inflammable material, which caught fire when van der Lubbe set to work; or—in an alternative version—they started the fires themselves. At the last minute, when all was ready, van der Lubbe was pushed through the window by some unknown and unseen companion, there to be picked up by the police. The compilers of the Brown Book also showed that van der Lubbe, far from being a Socialist of some intelligence, was a degenerate half-wit, and a homosexual prostitute, kept by the S.A. leader, Roehm.

This is the story that we all believed in 1933 and that most have gone on believing from that day to this. The evidence for it has now been examined by Herr Tobias. The result is like the Sheep's shop in *Alice through the Looking-Glass*:

> Whenever Alice looked hard at any shelf, to make out exactly what it had on it, that particular shelf was always quite empty, though the others round it were crowded as full as they could hold.

Each piece of evidence dissolves when closely examined; yet all the time you have the impression that the rest of the evidence must be solid. Take, for instance, the allegation that the firebrigades were deliberately delayed. This is disproved by the service-books at brigade headquarters. Again, nearly all the books say that the records of van der Lubbe's interrogations by the police have mysteriously disappeared. Herr Tobias found them at the office where they had always been —in eight copies. The blackening of van der Lubbe's character was peculiarly unscrupulous. After all, he had done something to show his enmity to the Nazis, which is more than the compilers of the Brown Book had done. They obtained a statement from a Dutch friend of his. One sentence read: 'I often spent a night in the same bed with him.' There was the proof of his homosexual character. As a matter of fact, the sentence originally went on: '. . . without observing any homosexual tendencies in him'. All the stories about van der Lubbe's bad upbringing, about his disreputable family, about his lack of friends, were in fact lies, Communist forgeries.

The vital evidence, however, was about the tunnel and its use by the party of Brown Shirts. This evidence was supposed to have been provided by unnamed Brown Shirts who repented and confessed secretly to the Communist exiles in Paris. One Brown Shirt appeared before the counter-trial,

muffled to the eyes. This was a wise precaution: he was in
fact a well-known Communist, and unmistakably Jewish. The
most important confession was not anonymous. It claimed to
be the work of Karl Ernst, Brown Shirt leader in Berlin. Very
conveniently it only turned up when Ernst was dead—killed
by Hitler in the great purge of 30 June 1934. Even more
convenient, Karl Ernst went out of his way to improve on
earlier versions, where these had been shown to be inaccurate.
For instance, the anonymous Brown Shirt informers had confessed that they were led by Heines, another Berlin Brown
Shirt chief. Heines was far away from Berlin, making an
election speech in his constituency, and this could be proved
from the newspapers. So Ernst kindly named himself as
leader. Again, the Brown Shirt men said they came through
the tunnel. Evidently they did not know that the tunnel was
lined with steel plates and that anyone going through it in
ordinary shoes made a noise like thunder; the night porter
would certainly have heard them. So Ernst added the detail,
surprisingly left out of earlier accounts that they all changed
into plimsolls.

There was one thing Karl Ernst got wrong. He agreed
with the other confessions that the Brown Shirts entered the
Reichstag at 8.40 p.m. This had to be the time if they were
to do their work before van der Lubbe was pushed through
the window at 9.03. Unfortunately, Ernst—or the Communist forgers—did not know one little event in the Reichstag routine. At 8.45 p.m. a postman came through the
side-door to collect the deputies' mail. On 27 February he
entered as usual; walked through the deserted building; and
left at 8.55 p.m. He saw nothing out of the ordinary—no
shadowy figures, no smell of petrol or other inflammable
liquid. The worthy postman, in fact, demonstrates the falsity
of all stories about the Reichstag which assume that there
was anyone present before van der Lubbe broke in at 9.03. It
seems equally unlikely that the Brown Shirts could have got
in at 9 p.m. and have escaped, their work finished, before the
police began to search the building at 9.22.

The mysterious tunnel presents some other odd features.

Immediately Goering arrived in the Reichstag building at 9.35 p.m., he exclaimed: 'They [the fireraisers] must have come through the tunnel.' He went off with policemen—not with Nazis—to examine it. They found the doors at either end securely locked. It was surely risky of Goering to search the tunnel if he was in the plot and knew that the Brown Shirts were on the way out. He and the police might have caught them. On the other hand, it was highly incompetent of the Brown Shirts, if there were any, to lock the doors. They ought to have left some indication of how the supposed Communists came in and went out. The very fact that no serious evidence was ever produced against the Communists really acquits the Nazis also. For if the Nazis had, indeed, set fire to the Reichstag, they would have manufactured evidence against the Communists—as the Communists later tried to manufacture evidence against them. All the evidence of the Brown Book breaks down, in its turn, on close examination. After all, it was not designed to be presented at a real trial. If it achieved a propaganda effect against the Nazis, Münzenberg and his assistants were satisfied. The more we look at the story, the clearer it becomes that, whatever else happened that night, no one came through the tunnel. There was no other way to enter the Reichstag, except past the night porter, or by breaking a window. No one went past the porter. Only van der Lubbe broke a window.

Those who have tried to defend the 'traditional' version are now inclined to admit that there is no clear or satisfactory explanation of how the Nazis got into the Reichstag. But they still point to the evidence of the experts at the trial that van der Lubbe could not have done it alone. Yet this expert evidence is the shakiest part of the story. The most emphatic expert was a crank distrusted by his colleagues. He claimed to be an authority on a strange 'fluid' which, he said, was necessary for starting fires. He alleged that this 'fluid' had a distinctive smell. No fireman, no policeman, noticed any smell except smoke—no 'fluid', not even petrol. Against this rigmarole, we can set the solid opinion of the police and of the fire-officers that van der Lubbe's story was perfectly consistent with the facts as they knew them. At first sight, it seems astonishing that one man could have set fire to this huge building. As a matter of fact, these gaudy public buildings burn easily. Dusty curtains, wooden panelling, high ceilings, draughts under the door—they were made for fires. In 1834 the Houses of Parliament at Westminster were entirely destroyed by fire, simply from one stove-pipe becoming too hot. Or if this be thought an antiquated story, the Vienna Stock Exchange was burnt out in 1956 as the result of one smouldering cigarette-end in a wastepaper-basket. Van der Lubbe had over twenty minutes in which to start fires. This was more than enough.

The conclusion is clear. Van der Lubbe could have set fire to the Reichstag by himself; there is a good deal of evidence that he did so; there is none that he had any assistants. Of course, new evidence may turn up to disturb these conclusions. So far, none has done so. There is one worrying point. The postman left the Reichstag at 8.55. Van der Lubbe broke in almost immediately afterwards, within a matter of minutes. How did he know when it was safe to break in? The only answer can be: he did not know. We have to assume a lucky coincidence, from his point of view. It is a smaller assumption than that demanded by any other story.

There has been an outcry in Germany, and still more in Communist countries, that Herr Tobias, by making this case, has whitewashed the Nazis. Even if this were true, it would be the fault of those who manufactured the Brown Book, not of Herr Tobias. That is the worst of forgeries: ultimately they come home to roost. But the new version does not, in fact, acquit the Nazis. Even if they had nothing to do with the fire, even if they genuinely believed that it was the work of Communists, this does not justify their subsequent illegalities and the reign of terror. They remain the evil men they always were. But the affair should change our estimate of Hitler's methods. He was far from being the farsighted planner that he is usually made to appear. He had a genius for improvisation, and his behaviour over the Reichstag fire was a wonderful example of it. When he became chancellor, he had no idea how he would transform his constitutional position into a dictatorship. The solution came to him in a flash as he stood among the smouldering ruins of the Reichstag that February evening. It was, in his own words, 'a heaven-sent opportunity', and we can agree with him that it came to him by chance from outside, though hardly from heaven. That is the way of history. Events happen by chance; and men then mould them into a pattern. Van der Lubbe set fire to the Reichstag; but the legend that the Nazis did it will probably prove indestructible.

XVI

UNLUCKY FIND

NAPOLEON used to ask of a man: 'Has he Luck?' Ability, experience, integrity were important; without luck they were useless. Neville Chamberlain had many great qualities. He had courage and industry. His intellect was clear and sharp. No politician this century has had a finer administrative brain nor used this gift better. When he became minister of health in 1924 he set out his reforming programme in 25 draft bills and carried 21 of them in the following four years. His Local Government Act of 1929, devised almost wholly by himself, had 115 clauses and 12 schedules. It shaped the structure of English local government to the present day. As chancellor of the exchequer, he recast the fiscal system, again with lasting effect. He commanded for a time the unquestioning allegiance of the Conservative party as none other of its leaders has done this century, not even Bonar Law. In Chamberlain's case, the allegiance was as strong on the front bench as among the rank and file. Yet it was all to no avail. The decisive element of luck was lacking.

Neville Chamberlain was without luck from the beginning. In the period of imperialist expansion, he stumbled on one of the few products, sisal, which failed to show a profit, and after five years of hard work in the West Indies came out with a loss of £50,000. In the first World war he was saddled with the hopeless task of organizing National Service, and failed again, though he was abler than most of those who reaped high honours. Lloyd George called him 'not one of my lucky finds'. When the Conservative leadership became vacant after the death of Bonar Law, Chamberlain found

ahead of him a man of few administrative or creative gifts,
easygoing and evasive: Baldwin, constantly threatened by
party revolt, yet repeatedly surviving, perhaps by innate
political skill, perhaps by the essential quality of luck.

Chamberlain's reforms were dwarfed by other events. Not
many cared about local government during the great depression; protective tariffs were less important in the 1930s
than quotas and currency management. As prime minister,
Chamberlain intended to be the initiator of domestic legislation. Instead he was caught by foreign affairs, and then led
his country lamenting into war. His fall was a further irony
of no luck. The Norwegian campaign was inspired and directed by Winston Churchill. Its failure brought down Chamberlain and put Churchill in his place. Even then Chamberlain
could have been in charge of administration at home. He
was struck by cancer, and died.

Neville Chamberlain has also been without luck after
death. He has had to carry the sole blame for the failure of
British foreign policy, despite protests from his more honest
colleagues such as Hoare. By now one would imagine that
Chamberlain conducted appeasement single-handed against
an almost unanimous Conservative and an entirely unanimous
Labour party. In 1946 Dr. (now Sir Keith) Feiling published
an authorized biography. This was soundly based on the
material then available: Chamberlain's letters to his sisters
and his rather dry diary. There was a full and carefully
drawn picture of Chamberlain's life in its various aspects,
though Dr. Feiling did not claim to be a specialist on the
period. The book attracted less notice than it deserved.
Maybe Englishmen were stunned by recent events, or did not
wish to disrupt the new national unity against Russia by
arguments about the past.

Still, Chamberlain's life was a subject which had been
covered. Apart from writing a polemical tract, a new biographer would need to strike a fresh hoard of private
material (or be able to prove that Dr. Feiling had suppressed
really important evidence). Alternatively, the new writer
would use the material published since 1946 from the official

records of the foreign office and the cabinet; he might even get permission to see records not yet published, as some others have done. Even without new information, he might provide a new perspective and show wisdom after the event. But once more: no luck. It is excessive even in Chamberlain's run of bad luck that a biography claiming to vindicate him should neither vindicate him in any serious sense nor contain new information of importance.[1]

Even an author who has been in the cabinet and, like so many figures now forgotten, a future prime minister has a duty to his readers; in this case a duty to explain why they should read a second biography when a first, satisfactory, biography exists. This duty is not performed. The earlier biography is not mentioned, though the name of Sir Keith Feiling appears occasionally in the text. There is no hint that the diaries and private letters have been examined before, and have already yielded practically everything. The most interesting quotations all appear in Feiling's book; indeed for the period when Chamberlain was prime minister there are many more of them. When Mr. Macleod has a new scrap to offer, this is produced with exaggerated emphasis. Thus a memorandum of 25 February 1931 from the Director of the Conservative Central Office, stating the dissatisfaction of the party with Baldwin as leader, is described as 'never before published'. Correct, but the gist is accurately summarized by Feiling.

Again Mr. Macleod prints in full from Chamberlain's diary the story of the events which led to Eden's resignation as foreign secretary in February 1938, and asserts that this 'makes clear much that has hitherto been conjectural and contradicts much that has hitherto been accepted'. In fact, Feiling printed five extracts from the account in Chamberlain's diary, which made the story clear, though passing over some details. Feiling's book is superior on nearly every point.

A few omissions are rectified. Feiling concentrated on Chamberlain and left out some episodes which might embarrass others, particularly when they were fellows of All

[1] Iain Macleod, *Neville Chamberlain*.

Souls. It is, for instance, odd that Sir John Simon, then a Liberal, should have drafted the Conservative vote of censure on the first Labour government over the Campbell case, when the Liberals were only asking for a committee of inquiry. Again, during the outcry over the Hoare-Laval plan, some members of the cabinet, including Chamberlain, felt that, since they had in fact endorsed the plan, they should not make a scapegoat of Hoare. One member of the cabinet however insisted that 'unless Sam went, the whole moral force of the Government would be gone'. Hoare went. In 1940, when Chamberlain proposed to move Hore-Belisha from the war office to the ministry of information, a cabinet minister objected that 'it would have a bad effect on the neutrals both because H.B. was a Jew and because his methods would let down British prestige'. As Mr. Macleod says, 'to all intents and purposes Hore-Belisha's career was broken'. On both occasions, the cabinet minister concerned was Lord Halifax. Such new information, though welcome, does not justify a book. Many writers have the experience at some time of taking up a subject which seems rewarding, only to discover that it has been adequately treated already. It is usual in such cases to abandon the subject with regret.

We might at least have expected that the passage of time would bring a more detached judgement, if not a more effective defence. In this, too, we are disappointed. There is little here which was not said better by Chamberlain at the time. Mr. Macleod does not much explore public opinion. He has a good quotation from the Labour spokesman at the time of the German reoccupation of the Rhineland:

It is only right to say bluntly and frankly that public opinion in this country would not support, and certainly the Labour party would not support, the taking of military sanctions or even economic sanctions against Germany at this time.

The speaker was Dr. Hugh Dalton. Generally Mr. Macleod is content to reiterate two points. First that 'Hitler was insatiable, war inevitable, and appeasement therefore a forlorn hope'; second, that Chamberlain, knowing the weakness of British armaments, was concerned only to buy time. Both points have become the current orthodoxy, so much so that any attempt to question them, or even to examine them dispassionately, is met not with argument, but with cries of abusive rage. Of course Hitler was bent, as other German statesmen had been, on making Germany again the dominant Power in Europe; and this undoubtedly made some war probable, if not inevitable, at some time. This is far different from saying that the war which started in September 1939 was inevitable, a war in which Great Britain found herself fighting Germany without any effective ally. Once Germany recovered from her defeat in the first World war, the only choice was between her domination over eastern Europe and Russia's; and the only clearheaded opponents of appeasement were those who preferred Russia to Germany. Most of those who condemn appeasement are even more indignant at the consequence of its failure, a consequence which was, in their own favourite word, 'inevitable'—the eclipse of the British Empire by Russia and America.

Chamberlain perceived some of this, though he did not perceive all of it. He certainly appreciated the weakness of British arms, and indeed exaggerated it. He supposed, as the experts did, that bombing was a decisive weapon and that more bombing was the only answer to it. Mr. Macleod waves aside the suggestion that Hitler was 'bluffing' in 1938. At this time, the Germans had 40 divisions, only one armoured; the Czechs alone had 36, four armoured. Hitler placed two divisions on his western frontier against 82 French divisions, and planned to send two more later. What was this if not bluff? It is too simple to say that Chamberlain merely aimed to buy time. He did this, but also hoped, and even believed, that appeasement might succeed.

Men, particularly statesmen, do not always think with precise and rigorous logic. Yet Chamberlain was not muddled or an appeaser by nature. On the contrary, he was more hard-headed than most of his contemporaries; he liked to get things settled one way or the other. At the beginning of the Abyssinian crisis, he was the cabinet minister most insistent for oil sanctions, though he was also the first to demand the ending of sanctions when they had obviously failed. Again, during the Abdication crisis, Chamberlain wished to present Edward VIII with formal cabinet advice to the King that he should end his association with Mrs. Simpson, together with a warning that the cabinet would resign if the advice were not taken. It was not that, as a Unitarian, he had religious principles against divorce; but the uncertainty was 'holding up business and employment'.

So, too, in foreign politics. Chamberlain did not have the emotional dislike of 'Versailles' common to most Englishmen at that time. He was merely irritated by the instability of the existing order, and regarded revision as an unpleasant necessity. And he was not taken in by Hitler. He found Hitler detestable, but not much more so than most foreigners except musicians. Chamberlain was neither blind nor stupid, least of all was he a coward. On the contrary, his courage was his undoing. He wanted to end uncertainty, to speed things up. In this he succeeded. His policy helped to produce in 1939 the war which everyone else, including Hitler and Mussolini, expected in 1943. His aim was to avert war. He failed; and failure on this scale cannot be excused by a plea of good intentions. Chamberlain is now beyond defence or condemnation. He needs a biographer who will try to understand him. Probably none will be found. Neville Chamberlain is fated to go on being the man of no luck.

XVII

DICTATOR WITHOUT A CAUSE

LAKE GARDA is an attractive place for a summer holiday. It gave a dreary exile to Mussolini and the ministers of the Italian Social Republic in the last 18 months of the war. The Germans were the real rulers of Italy down to the Allied lines. The Fascist government had nothing to do. The ministers studied reports, drafted decrees, discussed policy. Often Mussolini wearied of the pretence. Then he would get up and pace the room, reflecting on his destiny. He said: 'When I am gone the historians and psychologists will ask how a man had the power to lead such a fickle people as the Italians for so long.' This is a puzzle which no one has solved. The Italians were not merely fickle. They were politically mature, as they have shown since the second World war. They had political leaders of ability, fertile in ideas and skilful in tactics. Yet Mussolini held supreme power for almost as long as Sir Robert Walpole. Was it done solely by terror—castor oil and the Blackshirts? Not so. Mussolini came to power constitutionally with the approval of a majority in the Chamber; and the Fascists won two-thirds of the vote, to their own surprise, in a free election. For years afterwards Mussolini enjoyed a genuine and wide popularity.

This was not due to any solid achievement. No man has run a great state more incompetently. The finances were confused; the administration slovenly and neglected. Mussolini spent 18 years preparing for war. In 1940 Italy was worse equipped than she had been in 1915. He made no discoveries in economic policy. He put Italy back on the gold standard as blindly as Churchill did in England. He was caught unawares

by the great depression like any democratic statesman. The
Corporate State was a sham which never came to life. There
was no Italian New Deal, no Four or Five Year Plan. Mussolini admitted this himself. He said in one of his brooding
moments:

Fascism is Mussolini. As a doctrine it contains nothing new. It
is a product of the modern crisis—the crisis of man who can no
longer remain within the normal bounds of the existing law. You
could call it irrationalism.

The period between the wars seems, in retrospect, to have
had a special taste for rule by madmen. Hitler was not normal,
to say the least. Nor was he alone. Stalin became mad with
jealousy and suspicion, according to received Soviet doctrine.
Baldwin sat on the Treasury bench sniffing the order paper,
contorting his features, and cracking his fingers. Mussolini
himself remarked on this curious feature: 'Hitler and I have
surrendered ourselves to our illusions like a couple of lunatics.'

Though Mussolini surrendered to his illusions, he was not
taken in by them. He often recognized how little he had done;
how he failed to select competent men; how little he controlled the country over which he was supposed to dictate. He
was not surprised by failure, rather surprised that he had gone
on so long. The murder of Matteoti provoked a crisis of the
régime as early as 1924. Mussolini himself did not understand how he had overcome it. Similarly, he accepted defeat
at the Grand Council on 25 July 1943 as though he had
expected it for a long time. Yet he did not expect anything
serious to follow, and was bewildered to find himself out of
power, a prisoner. His rescue by Skorzeny surprised him just
as much: he had thought his life was over. Thereafter he kept
repeating: 'I must follow my destiny.' He knew what that
destiny was: to be killed and to be pronounced a failure. It
seemed to him the appropriate outcome.

Mussolini called himself 'a sort of mad poet'. Here he
judged wrongly. He was not a poet, by gift or even by temperament. He was an accomplished polemical journalist. He
devised headlines, and acted them. Everything he did was
for show, not for what followed. The great empty room at

the Palazzo Venetia with the great empty desk at one end impressed every visitor. The conversation after this first impression was commonplace. When Northcliffe drafted a peace programme at the end of the first World war, he was interested in the layout, not in the points which it contained, and Mussolini was just the same. He wanted material for a speech from the balcony. Once the speech was over he drew the curtains and went into a back-room to possess one of his innumerable mistresses. Though he loved his wife and was a good family man, his sexual appetite was insatiable. He seized every woman who came within range, and thrust her on to the floor. Most women enjoyed it, as most women enjoyed similar experiences with Lloyd George. Mussolini had little else to do in his days of power. He could not even write newspaper leaders. But his journalistic gifts never left him. Though he is supposed to have been physically decayed and almost senile before the end, the articles which he wrote on Lake Garda are as good as those which he wrote before the first World war. Their very title was brilliant: *The Year of the Stick and the Carrot.*

He is an attractive, and yet a baffling, subject for the biographer. There is plenty of material from which to draw his portrait as an individual. There is high drama before his rise to power, and after his fall from it. In the middle there is an enormous hole. Mussolini was ruling Italy all these years. What was he doing? Nothing except showing off. Two biographies show the difficulty well. Laura Fermi[1] is the widow of the famous nuclear physicist and a good writer in a simple, direct way. She lived in Italy until 1938. Then she and her husband moved to the United States. They had not noticed that anything was wrong with Fascist Italy. They moved only because she, though not her husband, was affected by the anti-semitic laws which Mussolini introduced to please Hitler. Later her eyes were opened. Now she tries to explain how Mussolini came to power and the evil things he did when he got it. The early part is admirable. She has worked over again the story covered by Megaro of Mussolini's days

[1] Laura Fermi, *Mussolini*.

as a socialist and of his conversion to nationalism. She goes carefully up to the so-called March on Rome. Then—emptiness. The murder of Matteoti, the Concordat, the conquest of Abyssinia, are all that she can find to record.

Mr. Hibbert puts the emphasis the other way round.[1] His book is the more dramatic and more exciting of the two. It is also more superficial. Slightly over half of it deals with the last 18 months of Mussolini's life after his fall from real power. This story is becoming an obsession with popular writers. We know every detail of the rival conspiracies which brought Mussolini down: the king nerving himself to action on one side, the dissident Fascists planning to jettison Mussolini on the other. The operation was as clumsily conducted as Mussolini's own strokes: everything botched, and the way left open for the occupation of Italy by the Germans. Thereafter Mussolini's movements are followed each day as schoolboys used to map the journeyings of St. Paul. The end on Lake Como is sensational, particularly as the killers of Mussolini left conflicting accounts. It needs music by Verdi to give it significance. In prose, it is just the killing of an old man and a romantic woman.

To the end, Mussolini carried round with him a bag of secret documents. What was in it? Apparently documents to prove how harmless and ineffective he had been: evidence that he had not inspired the murder of Matteoti; a letter from Hitler attributing the loss of the war to his attack on Greece; words of praise from Churchill. His pleas of innocence were not altogether unfounded. He had wanted to make a great impression, to manufacture headlines for tomorrow's paper. He did great evil only because others were so easily taken in by him. For him words were all that mattered. He was taken aback when action followed. The murder of Matteoti illustrated this. He inspired it less than Henry II inspired the murder of Thomas à Becket. On the other hand, characteristically, he did not atone for it. His foreign policy showed the same contradiction between words and acts on a larger scale. In private his judgements and impulses on foreign affairs

[1] Christopher Hibbert, *Benito Mussolini*.

were sensible and moderate from the days of Locarno until the time in 1943 when he urged Hitler to make peace with Russia. In public he could not resist ranting and roaring, though always in the hope that no action would follow. No great conqueror has gone to war more reluctantly or with less hope. Those who praised him—Churchill, Neville Chamberlain, Hitler—all discovered in him merits he did not possess. His redeeming feature was that he despised them for doing so.

Mussolini admired some of his opponents, though he used unscrupulous means to defeat them. He rescued Nenni from the Germans, and sent him to Ponza—soon to become Mussolini's own place of imprisonment. His early opponents had a poor record. They imagined that they could exploit him. Many Liberals, later of honourable standing, preferred him to the peril of Bolshevism—a peril which Mussolini had largely invented. There was a strange lack of resistance to the March on Rome. Perhaps most Italians were bored with Mussolini's uproar and thought that giving him power was the only way to keep him quiet. Somehow, too, the opposition missed their chance after the murder of Matteoti. Again, there was a strange indifference in their proceedings. The period of true dictatorship followed once Mussolini was on his feet. There was little opposition within Italy, though much abstention. Opposition became the politics of exile, always a thwarting subject. One emptiness opposed another. The Communists denounced their fellow exiles at one moment; thrust the Popular Front upon them at the next. Carlo Rosselli laboured to create a genuine movement of resistance, until he and his brother were murdered by French Cagoulards.

Resistance took on life with the Spanish Civil War. Guadalajara was an Italian victory as well as an Italian defeat. Here the real Italian resistance was born. It took on a more serious and effective character with the fall of Mussolini on 25 July 1943. Unlike some resistance movements, perhaps most, the Italians actually fought the Germans on a large scale. Mussolini performed one service to his country in falling as he did. The struggle became one of liberation, not of civil war. The resistance were no longer 'Mussolini's enemies'—who cared about Mussolini? They were the enemies of the Germans. The Allies performed another service to Italy when they treated the resistance with suspicion: no one could accuse the resistance of being Allied agents.

The men of the resistance were gravely disappointed at the end of the war. They had expected something more inspiring and more romantic. Yet the prosaic solidity of contemporary Italy is their true monument. The resistance redeemed Italian honour. Italy emerged from years of brutality and pretence as though Fascism had been no more serious than an attack of measles. This was really all it was. Mussolini was a bladder of wind, a malicious clown who strayed mistakenly into real life. He lived and died in melodrama. In Germany it is still possible to recognize that you are among the countrymen of Hitler. No one in Italy can suppose that he is among the countrymen of Mussolini.

XVIII

SPAM ON A GOLD PLATE

No one who lived through the Blitz of 1940 is likely to forget it: a terrible ordeal, but also a triumph of dogged courage. While women and children were evacuated by the thousand, everyone who had work in London, from cabinet minister to factory hand, stayed there and got on with his job. Among them was George VI. The king and queen, though sleeping at Windsor, commuted to London each day and endured repeated bombing at Buckingham Palace. Yet there was a difference between the king and his subjects. They had essential work to do in London; he attended at Buckingham Palace solely to be bombed. He could have gone through his 'boxes' just as well at Windsor or contributed more usefully to the war effort by turning shells on his lathe in the basement. This was the king's duty as he saw it: to share the sufferings of his people.

Mrs. Roosevelt, dining at Buckingham Palace in 1942, was given a meal 'which would have shocked the King's grandfather'. It was served on gold plate; and 'spam on a gold plate' would be a good motto for the reign. Another example. In 1947 George VI was in South Africa when the fuel crisis struck Britain. He wrote to Queen Mary:

> I am very worried over the extra privations which all of you at home are having to put up with in that ghastly cold weather with no light or fuel. In many ways I wish I was with you having borne so many trials with them.

Yet all the king could have done in England was to consume precious fuel.

Worry is the predominant note in the admirable, if somewhat courtly, biography which Sir John Wheeler-Bennett has written.[1] Before the Abdication of Edward VIII:

It is all so worrying and I feel we all live in a life of conjecture.

During the Munich crisis:

It is all so worrying this awful waiting for the worst to happen.

In the early days of 1940:

I am very worried over the general situation, as everything we do or try to do appears to be wrong, and gets us nowhere.

Only in June 1940 was there a cheerful note:

Personally I feel happier now that we have no allies to be polite to and to pamper.

This cheerfulness did not last. At the end of February 1942:

I cannot help feeling depressed at the future outlook. Anything can happen, and it will be wonderful if we can be lucky anywhere.

At the end of 1942, after Alamein and the landings in North Africa:

Outwardly one has to be optimistic about the future in 1943, but inwardly I am depressed at the present prospect.

Nor did victory improve matters for long. The King wrote in January 1947:

I have asked Mr. Attlee three times now if he is not worried over the domestic situation in this country. But he won't tell me he is when I feel he is. I know I am worried.

A few days later to Queen Mary:

I do wish one could see a glimmer of a bright spot anywhere in world affairs. Never in the whole history of mankind have things looked gloomier than they do now, and one feels so powerless to do anything to help.

Finally to Attlee in December 1950:

I have been very worried lately over affairs in general.

[1] John W. Wheeler-Bennett, *King George VI. His Life and Reign.*

George VI worried himself to death for the sake of his people; truly a sacrificial king, led as a lamb to the slaughter. Life imitates art, and George VI's reign reflected unconsciously the doctrines of Frazer's *Golden Bough*. No king has had a greater sense of duty, nor followed its promptings more strictly. This book inspires admiration for its subject, but also regret. The British were not aboriginal savages, despite the attempt of sociologists to treat them as such. They did not really want one man to die for the people. Though they were grateful for the king's sacrifices they would also have appreciated a king who had fun; and in the long run Edward VIII's waywardness may do as much for the monarchy as George VI's high principles. George VI had been trained to respect the throne, not to occupy it; and no man can change his character in mid-life. There is sincere indignation in the note of his first meeting with the Duke of Windsor after the Abdication:

He seems very well, and not a bit worried as to the effects he left on people's minds as to his behaviour in 1936. He has forgotten all about it.

George did not forget. Though he scotched Sir John Reith's proposal to introduce the former king as Mr. E. Windsor, he denied the title of Royal Highness to the duchess, and effectively prevented the return of the Windsors to England. George VI sustained the magic of monarchy.

Monarchy is also a practical affair, involved in the day-to-day workings of politics. Sir John Wheeler-Bennett provides much new information on this subject, some of a disturbing nature. The most important political act of a British sovereign is the choice of prime minister. It has been the last prerogative which he exercises without 'advice'. George VI did his best to let this prerogative lapse. It was on Churchill's advice, superfluous as it may seem, that he sent for Attlee after the general election of 1945. During the war, he worried over the possibility of Churchill's being killed on one of his trips abroad; and asked the prime minister to nominate his successor. Churchill 'formerly tendered advice' that the king should send for Anthony Eden. This satisfied George VI but not for long. Soon he worried again: what should he do if both Churchill and Eden were killed? Once more Churchill 'tendered advice'.

There can be no doubt that it is the Prime Minister's duty to advise Your Majesty to send for Sir John Anderson.

This surprising suggestion disturbs even Sir John Wheeler-Bennett's complacency.

One change of prime minister involved a real decision by the King. What should happen after the house of commons turned against Chamberlain in the early days of May 1940? Here was a rare moment for the king to voice the wishes of his people. On the contrary, George VI supported Chamberlain and sought to keep him in office.

It is most unfair on Chamberlain to be treated like this after all his good work. The Conservative rebels like Duff Cooper ought to be ashamed of themselves for deserting him at this moment.

The king offered to tell the Labour party 'that I hoped that they would realize that they must pull their weight and join the Natl Govt'—under Chamberlain's leadership. The resolute negative of Attlee and Greenwood saved the country from this dismal prospect. George then delegated the choice of successor to Chamberlain; and he in turn delegated it to a committee of four—himself, Halifax, Captain Margesson, and Churchill; a strange quartet to find the saviour of the country. Even on 10 May the king clung to Chamberlain: 'I was terribly sorry that all this controversy had happened.' Failing Chamberlain, the king wanted Halifax, 'I thought H. was the obvious man, & that his peerage could be placed in abeyance for the time being.' But H. 'was not enthusiastic'.

Then I knew that there was only one person whom I could send for to form a Government who had the confidence of the country, and that was Winston.

Such was the reluctance with which George VI appointed the man who was to be the greatest prime minister in British history. The episode does little credit to constitutional monarchy.

The king strove incessantly to keep up with political affairs. In the well-worn words of Bagehot, quoted again by Mr. Wheeler-Bennett, it was his right to be consulted; to encourage; and to warn. Chamberlain did not always trouble to observe the constitutional proprieties. The king first learnt of Eden's resignation in February 1938 from 'the Beaverbrook and Harmsworth press'. Later that year, Chamberlain announced his departure to Berchtesgaden in a casual postscript and forgot altogether to seek permission for his departure to Munich. Nevertheless he received wholehearted encouragement from the king. The Munich settlement had no warmer admirer than George VI. He shared, too, Chamberlain's distrust of Soviet Russia, and recorded of his conversation with Roosevelt in June 1939: 'He was definitely anti-Russian. I told him so were we.'

The constitutional maxim was slightly changed when Labour took office. Then George VI thought it his right to be consulted; to discourage; and to warn.

I told Attlee that he must give the people here some confidence that the Government was not going to stifle all private enterprise.

Again with Herbert Morrison:

We discussed the whole of the Labour programme. I thought he was going too fast with the new nationalizing legislation.

The king exercised decisive influence in one matter connected with the Labour government, despite its curious failure to leave a mark on Lord Attlee's memory. Of their first interview, the King recorded:

I asked him whom he would make Foreign Secy. and he suggested Dr. Hugh Dalton. I disagreed with him and said that Foreign Affairs was the most important subject at the moment and I hoped he would make Mr. Bevin take it. He said he would.

A memorandum made by the King's private secretary immediately after Attlee's audience confirms the story:

Mr. Attlee mentioned to the King that he was thinking of appointing Mr. Dalton to be his Foreign Secretary. His Majesty begged him to think carefully about this, and suggested that Mr. Bevin would be a better choice.

Attlee's lapse of memory began at once. When the king told the story to his new foreign secretary, Bevin replied that it 'was news to him'. So the country lost a foreign secretary who disliked the Germans, and a chancellor of the exchequer who knew something of economics.

In a longer perspective George VI's reign will mark the end of Empire. Ireland became a republic; and the King asked the Eire minister of external affairs: 'Tell me, Mr. MacBride, what does this new legislation of yours make *me* in Ireland, an undesirable alien?' India, too, became a republic; but then accepted the king as Head of the Commonwealth—by a strange twist, as Sir John Wheeler-Bennett observes, adopting De Valera's principle of 'external association' just when Ireland abandoned it. The Crown retained its position, but in an impersonal way. George VI never visited India; and it is difficult to believe that his visit to South Africa retarded republicanism. The coronation stone, or any other inanimate object, would do equally well as the symbol of association. For George VI, of course, these symbols had an importance. During the change in India, his main anxiety was when to abandon the 'I.' in his signature.

Against the record of withdrawal, there was one symbol of advance. George VI rescued the Garter from the prime minister of the day and made it 'non-political & in my gift'. Britain had lived through the most stirring years in her history. Never had so many citizens devoted themselves to public service. Whom would the king, of his independent will, delight to honour? The first list of his nominations contained the obvious warleaders. There followed in 1948: the Duke of Portland, Lord Harlech, the Earl of Scarborough, and Lord Cranworth. In 1951 there was a further batch: the Duke of Wellington, Lord Fortescue, and Lord Allendale. Who were these men? What had they done to deserve any honour, let alone the highest in the land? Did they even exist? They belonged to a world of shadows. In this world monarchy too had its being, and Sir John Wheeler-Bennett's eight hundred pages make it more shadowy still.

A. J. P. TAYLOR

A. J. P. Taylor was born in 1906 at Southport, England, and was educated at Bootham School, York, and at Oriel College, Oxford. He lived in Vienna from 1928 to 1930, where he learnt research from Professor A. F. Pribram. From 1930 to 1938 he was a lecturer in history at Manchester University and since 1938 has been a Fellow of Magdalen College, Oxford. He was Ford's Lecturer in English History at Oxford in 1956, Leslie Stephen Lecturer at Cambridge in 1961, and is a Fellow of the British Academy. He also gives television lectures, writes centre-page articles for the *Sunday Express*, and reviews books for the *Observer* and the *New Statesman*. Among his dozen books are *The Struggle for Mastery in Europe, 1848–1918* (1954); *The Origins of the Second World War* (1962); and *The First World War: an Illustrated History* (1963). He has just completed a final volume for the Oxford History of England, entitled *English History, 1914–1945*, and will now settle down to write the life of Lord Beaverbrook, of whom he was a close friend.